Zane Pre

The Re-Education of the Female

(A Book Every Woman Should Own and Every Man Should Read)

Dante Moore

SBI

Strebor Books

New York London Toronto Sydney

Strebor Books
P.O. Box 6505
Largo, MD 20792
http://www.streborbooks.com

This book is a work of fiction. Names, characters, places and incidents are products of the author's imagination or are used fictitiously. Any resemblance to actual events or locales or persons, living or dead, is entirely coincidental.

ISBN-13 978-1-59309-170-5
ISBN-10 1-59309-170-2
LCCN 2008925334

First Strebor Books trade paperback edition July 2008

Cover design: www.mariondesigns.com

10 9 8 7 6 5 4 3 2

Manufactured in the United States of America

For information regarding special discounts for bulk purchases, please contact Simon & Schuster Special Sales at 1-800-456-6798 or business@simonandschuster.com

DEDICATION

for the Sword!

ACKNOWLEDGMENTS

I would like to thank all the people who helped me through this process.

Lil D just for being my Prince.
Rasheedah (for being my friend).
Chandra Sparks Taylor (editor).
Brenda L. Thomas (author)—for your kindness and sound advice.
Khanequa (for all your help and support).
Professor Clarence "Tiger" Davis (for helping me regain my lost history).
And my spiritual father Dr. Khallid Abdul Muhammad (for bringing me out of the dark and into the light. For helping me become conscious).

TABLE OF CONTENTS

FROM THE AUTHOR

Wait! Before you get started, you need to read this first because after this page it starts to get real raw. Briefly consult the glossary if you're not familiar with slang. I wrote this book to educate and inform women about men, regardless of what you may think after you read it. I wrote in a form that shows the locker-room lingo that men use with one another if asked certain questions. The book is intended to show normal, everyday speaking written on a level that everyone can understand. I didn't intend to write every sentence in perfect grammatical form. I wanted women to read the truth from the mind of a man. I'm a masculine man, not some bitch-ass pansy who feels he has to relate to a woman's emotions in order to get his point across. I don't care about any of that.

I feel that the bond between African-American men and women is deteriorating rapidly, and I want to try to do something about it, but I don't want to be soft about it. I want to express my anger and frustration as a man with the women I feel are miseducated, misinformed, and ill-prepared about their responsibilities in getting and maintaining a relationship with a man of quality. I don't want to be nice about my delivery, I don't want to be subtle, and I don't want to dilly dally, pussyfoot, tap dance, tiptoe, or beat around the bush. I want to give you the truth straight out.

I'm not concerned with whom I may offend or hurt, and I don't give a damn if you like what I have to say or not. I think too many men are too passive about things when it comes to women to avoid hurting their feelings or starting unnecessary drama. But there's no line drawn when it comes to a woman hurting a man's feelings. She feels she has the full right to say whatever she wants, regardless of the impact it may have on a man's emotions. I also have this right. Within this book, I've tried my best to use that right to its absolute zenith. Please believe through editing that a lot more has been removed to make room for the book's core points. I think as men we shouldn't scale back our masculinity in order to connect with women. As a man, I'm independent, I take charge, and I'm in control. If a female doesn't understand or can't accept these things, then she needs to find herself an effeminate metrosexual or nowadays, another woman, who can better fulfill her needs. Neither I nor any other man should have to restrain our natural masculinity and dominant way of behaving because of a female's insecurities, anxieties, and idiosyncrasies. I feel if you start to subdue your behavior at the behest of a woman, it diminishes you as a man. So take a deep breath and relax, relate, and release all of those ill feelings and emotions you have toward men, and let yourself be educated, informed, and enlightened.

Later,
Dante...

PREFACE

This book is intended to educate females about a man's way of thinking when it comes to sex, relationships, and marriage. It is also meant to excite and entice readers into opening their minds to other possibilities when it comes to dealing with men and relationships. One of the author's main purposes is to provoke cognitive, conscious thinking between men and women when it comes to sex, relationships, and marriage. It is a waste of time to read the book and come away offended and combative and miss the author's main points. It is also important to understand that the author has purposely ignored mainstream standards to make the book a more compelling read. The author feels that books which have followed certain standards are boring and mundane and could have been much better reads if the original body of work was kept unchanged. This book is an excellent conversation piece, and you'll never grow weary of discussing the topics within.

OVERVIEW

Bitch, you got the game wrong, the Academy Award-winning Three 6 Mafia so eloquently stated on their *Choices* CD. This is the truth as I see it. The females of my generation have definitely got it wrong. They seem to think in regard to relationships they are in charge, running things, making moves and decisions. I'm here to tell you: slow your roll, sister, because you aren't in charge of shit. I'm about to break it down for you from a man's perspective.

1.) YOU AIN'T RUNNING SHIT

No respectable man with any kind of balls, heart, or masculinity is going to let you run him. He might let you think you're running things, but take it from me, a man who knows the game, you're not doing a damn thing but digging your own grave, figuratively speaking, of course. This is especially true for the African-American male. We are the ultimate alpha male, the pharaoh, the king of kings. Why would you think we'd let some woman run us?

2.) YOU AREN'T AN ANGEL OR A QUEEN

Bitch, please! Why would you think such a thing? Did God come down from heaven and place the precious ointment upon your head and anoint you as one of His angels? If He did, then I need to holla at you because I would like to see some shit like that. The only way to become a queen is to marry a king. So if you're already living like the wife of James Earl Jones in the movie *Coming to America*, then there's really no reason for you to be reading this book. But if you don't have maid servants, private chefs, and rose petals thrown at your feet, then I think you should shut the fuck up and read and be educated.

3.) I'M NOT DOING THAT

This could mean something sexual, something regarding hygiene or clothing, or maybe something concerning your home training or cleaning habits. Here's a little secret, ladies: men never really ask for anything. They command. When he says, "Baby, why don't you wear this?" or "What's for dinner?" do you think he's asking you to do that shit? Hell no. He's *telling* you. He's just trying to do it in a nice way. And if you come out your mouth with "I'm not wearing that" or "There's nothing for dinner. I didn't have time to cook," that shit gets filed in the back of our minds for future use. And believe me what *you* won't do, ten broads around the corner will.

4.) I DON'T NEED A MAN

Yeah, right. That's what women tell themselves as some sort of vindication because they can't get or keep a man. Loneliness will prove them wrong. Women who think this way are workaholics, alcoholics, Bible humpers, or drug addicted. They need somewhere to fill the empty void of not having a man. They try to keep themselves busy by becoming involved in frivolous activities, but the one thing they can't avoid is sleep. When it's time to hit the sack and they get under those covers cold, scared, and alone, they have to reach in their nightstand and pull out that vibrator and say to themselves, "I don't need a man."

I CAN'T TELL YOU EVERY DAMN THING

You have to figure some of this shit out for yourself. I couldn't fit everything I've learned about the female-male dilemma, the game, and relationships into one book. It would take volumes. The shit would be like *Encyclopedia Britannica*. The knowledge, hints, and ideas that I give you are not set in stone because of course, every man is different. You can move and shift around the tips and advice I reveal like pieces on a chess board. Mix and match to see what works best for you.

1

HOW TO GET A MAN

How does a woman get a man? Women have been posing this question to one another for many years, and maybe that's where the problem lies. They've been talking to one another when they should've been asking a man. If you want to know the truth, you go to the source. Women shouldn't listen to the misguided views of lonely, frustrated female friends; misinformed family members; overpriced therapists; or effeminate men.

How can a female get a man? Do you really want to know? It's very simple. Women just make it much harder than it is. Well, I'm going to give it to you straight from a man's perspective. Let's see if you can take it. You might be able to get through the book or you might not. Doesn't make a damn bit of difference to me either way, but if you do make it through, I guarantee that your perception of men will change and the way you go about trying to get one will, too, so let's begin.

APPEARANCE, APPEARANCE, APPEARANCE

You know how people say the first rule of real estate is location, location, location? Well, the same statement rings true for attracting a man, only it's appearance, appearance, appearance. I'm going to pound this into your head throughout this book. An attractive physical appearance is the number one thing you need to acquire and sustain in order to obtain and maintain a long-term relationship with a man you want and not someone for whom you've settled. Sometimes it's the only thing you need.

If you have weight issues; excessive body hair; poor hygiene; body odor; bad feet, teeth, or nails, then you need to handle that before you put yourself out there for a relationship. Ladies, if you don't do anything else—i.e. cook, clean, have a trust fund, a seven-figure salary, a multi-million-dollar business, or anything else that might accentuate you as a person—then the number one thing you need to do is take care of your appearance. The average man would rather have a broke, young, tight, cute chick with six-pack abs who works as a dishwasher at Rawlo's Pork Emporium than a fat-ass size twenty-four bitch who makes half a million a year. Don't believe me? Look around. How many fat, successful females do you see with boyfriends or husbands? Hardly any, correct? How many ditzy, brain-dead hookers wearing a size six do you see marrying the next big NBA or NFL star? They might not know how to balance a checkbook or what stock to invest in, but they know how to fuck, they know how to suck a dick, they're always wearing something sexy, and they know how to get and please a man. Nine times out of ten it's *your* man that they're getting.

A lot of women need to take notes. You can learn a lot just through observation. The most important thing you need to know when it comes to men is stay in shape and take care of your appearance. When I say stay in shape, I mean exercise regularly and don't be a size eighteen. For Black women you should try to keep yourself under a size ten, unless you're at least five-eleven. The entire African race is born large, and there's nothing we can do about it, so don't even worry yourself about that. Genetically, we are the largest humans on the planet, and we're born with the most defined muscle tone. It's been that way since antiquity, and it's not going to change. As a matter of fact, the African race has been getting even larger over the years.

A size ten might be large for an Asian, Hispanic, Indian, or White chick, but for African-American women, it's a more than acceptable size. You shouldn't be trying to look like an Asian or Caucasian anyway so just worry about what's attractive for an African-American woman. If you're trying to attract a man who isn't African-American, then you need to be even smaller.

As an African-American woman, or any woman for that matter, the fatter you get, the more you decrease your potential single-man pool. Let me give you an example. When you go to the grocery store to shop, do you pick out the nastiest-looking, most rotten, smelliest fruit or meat you can find? Oh, you don't? Why not? Why don't you try eating the disgusting-looking food first, then decide whether it tastes bad or not? Because any fool can see that the food is bad, so why eat it?

It's the same with men when they see baby elephant-sized, out-of-shape women. They see your big ass when you waddle into the club, bar, church, grocery store, or wherever. Why are they going to try to start a conversation with you when it's blatantly obvious that you don't even care how you look on the outside? An obese outward appearance is a clear sign that something is wrong internally. At the very least, it's a lack of self-discipline. If you don't care how you look on the outside, a man can just imagine what's on the inside. Just like the rotten fruit, if it's rotten on the outside, what makes you think it's going to taste good when you bite into it?

This is the type of logic that so-called BBW (Big Beautiful Women) or full-figured women use to justify their appearance. They say shit like, “He should get to know me and not judge me solely on my appearance.” Why? Why should a man try? Did God make Eve fat and ugly? No, he didn’t because he was creating an example for all women to follow. Learn to control your appetite and exercise. Stop trying to take the easy way out, wanting men to accept you when you are grossly overweight. Then you complain to your girlfriends that you can’t find a good man and there aren’t any out there. There are good men everywhere. They just don’t want your big ass. Men have standards, too, especially when it comes to making someone their wife or girlfriend. Ours are more rigid than a woman’s simply because we have far less of them. They may be something like she can’t weigh more than me, she has to be fairly cute in the face, and she has to have good hygiene. Do you see how these standards must be met? The average man, I’m sure, has more requirements. I just mentioned those to give you a basic understanding of how we think.

A woman’s standards may be something like his shoes have to be expensive and clean, he must be college educated, make as much or more than I do, be at least six-two, have his own place, have an expensive car, not have any kids, love animals, love his mother, believe in Jesus Christ or have some sort of religious belief and go to church, have all his hair and, if he has hair, then it can’t be longer than mine, all his teeth must be straight, he must be clean cut, and he must be a Democrat. I could go on but I think you get the point. Do you see how a woman can be more flexible on her requirements? It’s possible that a man may fit a woman’s many requirements, but if a woman doesn’t fit his three, then that’s a done deal. He won’t move forward with the relationship. He will fuck you, though. A man wants a female he can be proud to have on his arm. Not some chick that will gnaw it off if there isn't any food readily available. Someone he can take around his friends and family and not be ridiculed. Just because he doesn't see you as a wife doesn't mean he won't have sex with you. Men separate sex and love. In their minds one has nothing to do with the other, and they're always on the prowl for some good twaka. Some good pussy from a fat chick, who no one is ever going to see you with, is better than no pussy at all.

For you big women, I'm sorry to be the one to tell you, but if you're using terms like *full-figured*, *big beautiful woman*, *curvy*, *pleasantly plump*, *thick*, or *voluptuous* to describe yourself, then you're just plain fat, and you need to lose weight, point blank, period. Yeah, you might look good enough to fuck, but that's about it. Most of the men you've met, I'm pretty sure have used you and thrown you away like a soiled Kleenex. This I know because I'm one of the muthafuckas who did you like that. I've met countless five-six, 195-pound females whining about how there are no good men out there or men ain't shit or they're not changing for any man. They say shit like, "If he won't love me the way I am, then I don't need him." Do you know how much I laugh to myself when I hear shit like this? I have to stop myself from laughing right now as I'm typing this. Get real! Everybody changes.

If you're dating a man and you think he's a potential husband, and you're a smoker and he wants you to stop smoking, then you're going to put that cigarette down. You won't let a simple thing like a bad habit ruin a potentially lifelong relationship. If you would, then that's your stupidity.

This book can only teach. It can't think for you. Like someone once said, you can lead a horse to water but you can't make him drink. For you big women, put the sausage down and let me flip the script for a second. Stand in front of a full-length mirror while you do this little exercise. Pretend that you're a man like Blair Underwood, Boris Kodjoe, Idris Elba, the cute guy at your job, or whomever you desire. As you're pretending to be that man, ask yourself, *Would I stop to talk to this broad in the mirror?* I'm not going to answer the question for you because you know the answer. On second thought, I guess I will answer my own question. Hell no! What makes you think he's going to walk past that young broad with the phat perky titties, a flat stomach, cute face, and phat ass to talk to your big ass? I'm not trying to make you cry or break you down. I'm just stating the truth and what's real. I'm giving you the truth straight out. If you can't take it or don't like it, then put the book down, go to your room and cry. But if you want to know more, then take a deep breath and keep reading. Yeah, he might talk to you and get to know you because he sees you as a quick fuck, one of his broads he can call at three a.m. after the club closes to get some pussy, then bounce. He may even take you out and date you, or lead you on to think that you're in a relationship, so he can fuck whenever he wants and receive the perks that go along with being considered your man. But believe me, that's as far as it will go. After he starts tapping that ass, there's no more need for you. To him a wife you will never be. If you tried you could be that perky-titty, flat-stomach, cute-face, phat-ass chick, so stop being lazy and handle that business. Eat healthy and exercise regularly. You should be doing this anyway for your general health and well-being. Appearance is what you need to initially grab that man's attention. If you don't have an attractive appearance, then you're just another face in the crowd.

ADVERTISING AND MARKETING

Men are very visual, so you have to show off the goods, sweetheart. When you go shopping at a grocery store, you have so many of the same items to choose from. What makes you pick one particular item? Is it the name on the package? Is it the bright colorful wrapping? Is it the bold words that jump out at you? Maybe you heard about the item from a friend. But for whatever reason, you choose one. You must apply these same techniques in getting a man. Get your physical appearance in order and show it off. You don't have to dress like a hooker. Just make sure you stand out enough to get noticed. Tell your friends that you're looking for a potential mate and to introduce you to some men they know are available. I know there are some jealous broads out there who will never do this for any female, and they will also try to cock block the action you do get. However, if she's really your girl and she really has your best interest in mind, she'll try her best to hook you up without a second thought.

Don't think of these acts as desperate. These are actually very subtle. I've recently heard about several men using billboards to get dates. One was an African-American Harvard business graduate. I don't think these men are desperate at all. I think the idea is brilliant. In one shot they've used the money they would've spent on dating services, bars, clubs, Internet dating, and other gimmicks in combination with their own ingenuity and instantly improved their dating odds. If billboards were inexpensive, I'm sure you'd see hundreds of them used in this capacity. What is an Internet dating profile besides a computerized billboard? People are busy and they have other shit to do. It's hard to have a social life while working sixty hours a week. You need to let people know that you have your physical appearance in order and your shit together and you're available, or else how would they know?

Let me give you an example. If you invented a great product, let's say for instance, the cure for cancer. Would you just sit outside your home trying to sell it and in very small print have "cure for cancer" at the bottom of the bottle? No! You'd have billboards, radio ads, TV commercials, wristbands, key chains, T-shirts, anything you could think of to inform people of this product. Why wouldn't you do the same for yourself? If you have your physical appearance in order and your priorities straight concerning men, you should consider yourself a great product.

To get a man you just can't go to work and come home. Then maybe on the weekends you hit the club with your girls and expect to find a single, professional man. You have to make yourself available to be approached or to initiate an approach almost everywhere you go. If you want to grab a quick bite to eat, don't just go to the drive-thru; get out of the car and go in. You never know; you might find something in there you like besides the chicken sandwich. If you go to the Blockbuster to drop off a movie, don't just throw it in the quick-drop and keep rolling. Take it inside and look around. You never know; you might find something in there besides your favorite flick. Do you see where I'm going?

Take your time and explore. How are you going to meet anyone sitting at home talking on the phone to your girls about how bored you are? Get out and do something. Don't just make it a girls' night out, either. Make a point to go out and meet men. Challenge yourself and your female friends. When you *do* decide to go out, don't just go to places that *you* want to go to. Go to places that you know men frequent. Local sports bars are always popular with males. Places where there is competition like pool halls, and advanced video game facilities like ESPN Zone, Jillian's, and Dave & Buster's are known for attracting men. Check these places out for yourself, and ask your male friends where they like to hang out. If you don't mind people at your house, then you can set up small gatherings, speed-dating events, or discussion forums where you only invite single available men and women. One place that I don't think women know much about is local boxing matches. Some places call it ballroom boxing. You probably won't hear about the match on TV or radio but if you live in a city that has boxing such as mine, then try to attend one. They are inexpensive, and they occur often. Promoters, current and former boxers, trainers, lawyers, advertising execs, musicians, and businessmen all attend. Some nights it is packed to capacity. It's an untapped resource that you can use to your advantage. Don't say to yourself, *I don't like boxing. It's too brutal.* Who cares! You're not there to watch the fight. You're there to prance your cute ass around and to try to get some attention from men. So do it.

A lot of women seem to go places where there are lots of other women. I guess they figure if there are women there, men will be there to. This is somewhat true, but I think you'd dramatically increase your odds of meeting a man by lowering the competition. Try places where you know there will be lots of available men but not many women. All of these are just suggestions. The point is to get out and get active in trying to meet someone. You're never going to meet anyone sitting in the house complaining and feeding your face. Market and advertise yourself accordingly.

BEEP BEEP HEY TOOT TOOT

Females ask me all the time, "Why do men beep the horn when they're driving and keep going?" Most of them pose the question like they're offended that someone has beeped at them. Why do you think men do this? Because they want to meet women, but they've got shit to do. Most of the time they're on the opposite side of the street, and they just want to acknowledge that the woman they're beeping at is attractive. If they're on the same side of the street as you, then they'd probably slow down and beep the horn to get your attention. A lot of men beep and wait for a response. If you're walking and some man beeps at you and you respond by slowing down, waving, stopping, or looking around to see who did it, then most of the time the man will make a U-turn and come back to talk to you. Don't dismiss the fact that somebody has beeped the horn at your stinking ass. Take it as a compliment because there's going to come a time in your life when nobody will ever beep at you again except to tell you to get the fuck out the way.

I was watching a behind-the-scenes special on the rap artist Ludacris one evening. He was performing in his hometown of Atlanta. Before the show, the camera crew followed him all around the city while he did his daily activities. Just before showtime they filmed him getting dressed at a friend's house. When he was ready to go, Ludacris and two friends hopped into an ordinary car, and they headed to the spot where he was supposed to perform. Ludacris was in the back on the passenger's side. When they got close to their destination, they noticed two attractive females walking toward where the event was to be held. They slowed down and honked the horn. The females ignored them. They did it again. The females ignored them. They slowed down to the females' walking speed, and beeped the horn again while trying to have a conversation with them. The females didn't respond. It wasn't until Ludacris put his head out the window and said something that they started screaming and running toward the car. Ludacris and his friends pulled off and he said, "You should've stopped when we beeped." That was a once-in-a-lifetime missed opportunity for those two women. You never know who might be beeping at you to get your attention.

Do you know that on a nice day men purposely ride around the city just to meet women? This is not something that's done willy-nilly. This is done with a defined purpose. Remember men are action-oriented. Two or more men aren't going to ride around the city for nothing. The reason is to meet women, and the person in the passenger seat has the most important job—to look around, find women and direct the driver to their location. Once they've reached the female's location, then it's the passenger's job to initiate the conversation. Of course if they arrive at the female's location and they're on the driver's side, then starting the conversation becomes the driver's job. A lot of the time the passenger is the owner of the car but he has designated one of his friends as the driver so he can get first dibs on the females they meet.

Stop listening to the TLC song "Scrubs" because both of those chicks are single. One group member's marriage lasted a hot minute and now she's divorced and the other one got some confessions from her X man. If the passenger tries to talk to you, don't dismiss it. Remember a lot of times someone who is being driven is someone with prestige. Once you've attained a certain financial status, cleaning and driving are the first two things to go because either you have the financial means to pay someone else to do it or you just don't have the time to do it yourself. You never know who's in the passenger seat. If he's your type, then you better grab that opportunity when he tries to talk to you. Don't miss out on your husband because you're caught up with what some single broads said in a song. Wouldn't it be funny if your husband did turn out to be in the passenger seat when you first meet? You would be able to laugh about it with him years later. It wouldn't be so funny if you snubbed him and years later your ass is still alone.

STOP WAITING FOR EVERYTHING TO COME TO YOU

Have you ever heard the old sayings, "You snooze you lose," "the early bird catches the worm," "the squeaky wheel gets the grease?" Do you know what they mean? They mean, "Don't wait for every man to come to you." Go out there and make an effort to find your man. Just don't sit there and expect shit to drop in your lap. "Get off your ass." When you see something you like, make a move, "speak up." Something simple like "hello" is a good start. Do you apply them when it comes to getting a man? Tell me this, why do women say shit like "I'm waiting on the right man" or "If the right man is out there for me, God will reveal him." Are you fucking crazy? Didn't God wait like four hundred years to free the slaves in Egypt? If you had a winning lottery ticket, would you wait until after it expired to cash it? If you were standing in the path of a speeding car, would you wait for someone to push you out of the way to keep from being hit? If you knew the answer to the final question on *Who Wants to be a Millionaire*, would you get off the podium and just walk away with nothing? All of the answers to the previous questions should be "no." If you wouldn't wait for these things, then why would you wait for a man to come to you?

You better get off your ass and make a concentrated effort to get your man. Nothing is just going to fall in your lap. Life is not a fairytale where you wait for Prince Charming to slay the dragon and come save you. If you want a man, you have to put yourself out there like you're looking for one. The first way to do this is by getting your appearance in order. If you're fat, then lose weight. If you have bad skin, then you need to see a dermatologist. If you have no ass and have a flat chest, then get a padded bra and do some squats to perk up that ass. I hear they even have injections now that you can take to pump up that ass. Everybody wants to be Black. Like comedian Paul Mooney once said, "Everybody wants to be a nigga but nobody wants to be a nigga." Anyway, whatever you feel you're lacking, try to improve appearance-wise and accentuate the positives you do have.

You need to talk to any man who speaks to you. By doing this you give off a friendly disposition, and it keeps you in practice on how to talk to men and how to have a general conversation. Now I'm not saying you have to carry on a twenty-minute conversation with someone you're not interested in, but if he speaks to you, then you need to speak back. The reason for this is if you're not interested in him, another man may be watching who's your type and may not speak or approach you because you gave off a snotty attitude. Men do this all the time. A man will watch you as you walk into a room or wherever. You don't see him but he sees you. He's your type, and he thinks you're attractive and wants to talk to you. You're walking his way, and he's getting ready to get your attention when all of a sudden another man approaches you and tries to talk to you. He's not bad-looking but he's not your type, so you catch an attitude and act like a bitch and keep on stepping with your nose in the air. The other man who was your type and about to talk to you turns his back and walks away. You go home alone once again with your pussy in dry dock wondering why no one tried to talk to you in the library, subway, grocery store, club, or wherever. The reason why is because you gave off the bitch vibe or you showed your ASS—Angry Sista Syndrome—as described in a post by Jamal Sharif.

I know you've seen this before. An attractive woman is walking down the street and a man speaks to her. He doesn't say anything rude, just a normal "Hi, how are you?" The woman completely snubs him like he doesn't exist. You've probably seen this and said to yourself, *How rude*. You might have done this yourself. Men see this also. Some men even key in on it. They seek out a woman who acts like this so they can talk to her, get her number, and treat her just like she acts—a bitch. I mean, really, who wants to talk to someone who acts like a bitch, be it male or female?

Let's revisit this scenario. We will begin with the guy who's not your type approaching you. Instead of being rude about the whole situation, you politely smile as if you're surprised that anyone would even want to talk to you. He asks for your number, and you give some lame excuse why you can't give it out. "I just moved and my phone isn't on yet." If he offers you his number, accept it. You don't have to call. After that gently slide away and keep stepping. Or you can stand there and listen for a minute to what he has to say and then give him a blank. You can even give him your real number, then when he calls let him know that you just want to be friends. You never know what can happen when you open yourself up to being approached. He just might have a friend he can introduce you to who turns out to be your future husband. There are dozens of ways to successfully exit this situation without being a "bitch" about it. Most women whom I've observed choose the "bitch" way out.

As I've said before, men are very visual, and they're extremely observant when it comes to women. Believe me, you might think no one's looking at you but if you have your body and appearance in order, believe me they're looking. When a man observes the first scenario where the woman snubs the guy, then he's going to say to himself, *Oh, she's a real bitch. There's no reason for me to even try to get to know her*. But if he watches the second scenario unfold, then he's going to say to himself, *Oh, she seems open. Maybe that dude just wasn't her type. Well, I think I'll try my hand.* Remember the old saying, "You can catch more flies with honey than you can with vinegar"? That shit is true. You better listen. If you give off a bitch attitude, then that's what men will treat you like—a bitch.

BE AGGRESSIVE

When I say be aggressive, this doesn't mean you have to act like a man. You can be demure and still be aggressive. When most women go out, they do absolutely nothing but sit around and show off the goods. They expect everything to come to them. They expect men to approach them, buy them drinks, start and end the conversation. This is the wrong attitude to have if you're trying to find a man because even the finest women sometimes get overlooked. Have you ever been out with your girls and for some reason you were getting all the attention from men? They just seem to approach you all night. You felt like a superstar that night. Then the next time you and the girls go out the men are all over one of your girlfriends and no one is even looking at you? That's just how it is sometimes when you're passive. One night it may be *her* night and the next it may be *yours*. If you're aggressive, then *every* night will be your night.

Being aggressive as a woman is a lot different from being aggressive as a man. As a woman you can do little things like making eye contact, winking, smiling, waving, looking his way just a little too long, or doing something else small that indicates you're interested.

A lion doesn't need any provocation to attack, but if you're dangling raw meat in front of its face, the odds of you being attacked are pretty high. The same goes for a man. Let's say there are two women a man is interested in and he makes eye contact with both. One smiles and waves when he looks her way and the other doesn't. Odds are he'll approach the one who's smiling and waving. Sounds simple, right? Either a lot of women don't know, don't care, or don't utilize these small techniques.

A lot of Bible-humping women will read this and say, "It says in the Word that the man is supposed to pursue the woman." That's cool if you believe that bullshit. You can stop reading now and go curl up in the bed *alone* holding your Bible. Remember the Bible says a lot of things. I will get deeper into this in another chapter. I'm pretty damn sure you won't go to hell if you approach a man and start a conversation. If I'm wrong then holla at me when we're both in purgatory, and I'll apologize for the entire situation. Until then, put the Bible down. keep reading this book and focus. There's nothing wrong with approaching a man and starting a conversation. You can take the advice of the Bible-toting broad who is probably home alone every night pleasuring herself, sit back and do nothing, or you can do something about your own situation.

Black women, you need to especially take heed: I am definitely into my sistas, but I've been approached by more White, Latino, Puerto Rican and Asian females than I ever have sistas. Sistas have been so brainwashed that they think it's a bad thing to go up to a man and start a conversation. How silly is that? Black women, I know you've heard this next saying to the point where it's beginning to sound cliché and the reason why is because the shit is true. You have bad attitudes. Your attitudes stink when it comes to men. That's why you get treated so badly by some Black men—because of the way you act. In my experience, when it comes to women of other races, they're easier to talk to, and a lot of times they'll approach you. When you talk to Black women, during the first few questions of the conversation, they want to know what you do, what you drive, where you live, and where you plan on going with your career aspirations. When I talk to women of other races they want to know what you're doing later on, when they can see you again, what type of things you enjoy doing, or when they can make you dinner or do something for you. They're not concerned with that other bullshit. They're genuinely interested in you. They don't mind paying for the first date or any date because they just want to be with you.

A Black woman always wants to know what you can do for her. I can tell you what men can do for you—nothing but give you some dick. That's the way some men think when you come off acting bourgeoisie and stuck-up, when in reality you ain't nothing but a glorified secretary with a nice job title.

Don't you know that a man will fuck you just for spite? When you meet a man and you start saying little smart shit, he's thinking, *As soon as I fuck this bitch, I'm going to treat her like garbage because she definitely thinks she's like that*. How many times has this happened to you? You meet a man and as soon as you have sex with him, he starts acting different? It's because of all the bullshit you did to him before he fucked you. You say to yourself, *He was so nice and romantic before we had sex and now he talks so bad to me and acts like he doesn't want to be bothered with me anymore.* Sound familiar? Well, wake the fuck up. Why do you think this is happening? Do you think all men act like this? Do you think this is how all men are, their natural nature? Wrong, bitch. It's you, and it has always been you. Take a look at what you're doing to have this happen to you, and if you can't find anything, then look again because believe me, it's there.

If you want to get a man, then act like you want to get a man. Don't bullshit. Don't get all dressed up in heels, a tight skirt, low-cut blouse, and thong, and go out, and when someone tries to talk to you, you say some dumb shit like "Oh, I didn't come here to meet anyone." That's bullshit and you know it. If you're one of those females who calls men "dogs" all the time, then you should already know how sensitive a dog's nose is. The average dog can smell a female dog in heat up to a mile away. If a dog can smell pussy a mile away, then don't you think it can smell bullshit, too? If you didn't come out to meet anyone, you could've stayed in and not met anyone in your own damn house or section eight apartment. You could've made perfectly sure that you didn't meet a damn soul by staying your ass right at home, feeding your face in front of the TV. Don't ruin your chances of meeting someone by having the wrong attitude.

I was talking to this female I'd met at the gym. She was one of those people you see at the gym but nowhere else. Well, one day I was out at this club, and I happened to run into her. I spoke to her and went about my business. The next time I went to the gym, she asked, "Did you have a nice time?"

I said, "Yes, I enjoyed myself. What about you?"

She said, "I'm never going back there again."

"Why?" I asked.

"I just don't like to be hounded like that."

I thought, *Well, why the hell did you even go there*?

She goes to the gym every day, and she has a gorgeous body. If you don't want men to be attracted to you and talk to you, then go to a gay male club. This way you can be surrounded by men who won't approach you. You better use it before you lose it and flaunt it while you got it. Like I said previously, there's going to come a time in your life when *no* man will ever hound you again. That's when you'll pray for even the slightest attention from any man.

If you're going out with your girls, tell them, "Girl, I'm trying to meet every single available man I can." If she's really your friend, then she'll listen and try to hook you up. If she isn't your friend, then she'll get mad at the attention you're getting and want to go home early. Or she won't send any action your way or cock block any attention you might already be getting. You don't have to fuck the men you meet. All you're trying to do is get to know them. It doesn't make you a freak, slut, loose, or whatever, just because you flirt with various men. If you're not fucking any of them, then who cares how many men you talk to? If you do go out with your girls, make sure you give yourself sufficient time away from the group to mix and mingle. Men prefer to approach women who are alone and not standing together with five of their homegirls. It's just like a predator staking its prey. The predator (usually the man) will wait until his prey (usually the woman) wanders away from the herd, and then attack suddenly at the first open opportunity.

Men do this because if there's a group of women and a man is interested in meeting more than one, and the woman whom he initially approaches is alone but isn't interested, then he can approach the others in the group at a later time without the rest knowing about it. But if he approaches the women while they're in a group and the woman he tries to talk to isn't interested, then usually the remaining women won't talk to him because he tried to talk to one of their friends first. Silly, isn't it? Yeah, but that's what you broads put us through. So these are the type of measures men have to take to ensure success in the dating game.

I've spoken with a lot of Black women, and the consensus for not approaching a man seems to be they're afraid of rejection. Most have never approached a man. I try to get them to understand that being turned down is a part of life. If you were in a relationship that didn't work out and you weren't the one to end it, then you've been rejected. That man didn't want you for some reason, so you need to get over that rejection shit quick. Men get turned down all the time and keep coming back for more. If all the wrong men are approaching you, then why wouldn't you approach one you think may be right for you? If you do decide to approach a man, don't say little dumb shit like "Do you have the time?" and then stop talking and expect him to catch on to that you're trying to flirt with him. The last thing a man is thinking when a woman approaches him is that she's trying to holla at him. So if you're going to approach a man, you might as well put it out there. You got past the hard part of walking up to him and starting a conversation. There's no need to blow it by not getting your point across. Women are very subtle when it comes to shit like letting a man know they're interested. Men usually don't notice those subtleties or the small hints you're directing toward them.

I'll tell you a little story from my past and the subtleties of one woman I encountered. I had just moved to this new apartment complex. I'm kind of friendly at times so usually I will say hi to women or people I encounter. I was at the complex for about three months, and I'd had several conversations with various females, but I hadn't tried to talk to any. One day I came out to my car and I saw a note on my windshield that read: "we spoke to each other several times. Just wanted to know if you were interested." It was signed "Ms. Prix." The first thing that came to my mind was that one of my homeboys was playing a joke on me. Then I thought about if further and realized that playing a joke like this wasn't their style. So I thought, *Ms. Prix? Who in the world could I have spoken to and made such an impression?* I figured since she gave her last name, she would be pretty easy to find.

I went to the complex's mailboxes, checked the names and the name Prix was nowhere. I kept the letter for a few days, still going about my daily business. But now my awareness was a little more heightened. Nothing new happened, and I kept seeing the same females and neighbors I'd usually seen. After a while I threw the letter away, thinking that it might have been a joke after all. About a month passed, and I was outside of my complex cleaning my car. Another car pulled up beside mine and a woman stepped out. She approached me and said, "After you're done with that one, you can start cleaning mine." I thought that was kind of funny at the time so I laughed, and we began talking. I'd seen her around the complex on occasion, and we seemed to always park beside each other. After a while I got her number, started calling her, and we began dating. After a few dates, she revealed that she was the one who had left the note and wanted to know why I didn't respond.

I said, "You were the one that left the note, but your last name isn't 'Prix.'"

She said, "I signed the note 'Ms. Prix' because I drive a Grand Prix, and we park beside each other all the time. I'd never done anything like that before, and I thought you would pick up on it."

I thought, *Now how was I supposed to put that shit together?* A woman whom I'd met briefly leaves a note and signs it using her car as a last name. I'm supposed to be like, *Oh yeah, I know who that is.* Please. I didn't know who the fuck had left the note, and if I hadn't started seeing her, I would've never found out. But do you see how subtle that was? To a woman that is probably a huge clue but to a man it's like a needle in a haystack.

THE SWIFF

I am going to touch on this briefly because I haven't done enough research on it to know if it's just localized in the Washington, D.C. metro area. The palm scratch, also called "the Swiff," consists of two rough scratches in the center of the palm. The hand of the individual who is scratching is usually on the bottom and the partially open palm that's being scratched is on top to conceal what's happening. It can be either way. It's basically used after first meeting someone. After you've greeted the person and have shaken hands, upon initial separation of the handshake, you deliver the two scratches before complete separation occurs. The reason that they're two scratches and both must be rough is to make perfectly clear that it wasn't an accident.

The Swiff is mainly used in the nightclub scene, but it also can be used outside of it. Outside of the club, it's a covert way to let a person know that you're very interested in getting to know him or her. It bypasses all the bullshit and gets straight to the point. You don't have to introduce yourself, or make polite conversation or witty banter. The Swiff is the equivalent of all of this. Inside the club it means the person wants to fuck, but everyone doesn't take it to mean that. Most people take it to mean, *I like you, I'm interested in you, I would like to get to know you better, I want your number,* things like this. You can use this to your advantage when you're introduced to a man. You can use it when you're getting change from a bartender, cashier, or shaking hands with a newly introduced male, coworker, or whomever. Any time hands briefly touch, the Swiff can be used. This is a subtle but extremely effective way to let a man know you're interested without saying a word. The only disadvantage is if he doesn't know what it means, then he won't be aware of your intentions. Usually scratching someone's palm twice would pique interest, so if he doesn't know what it means, you can just explain it to him when he inquires. Either way it's a win-win situation for you.

STOP THINKING YOU'RE ALL THAT

Halle Berry, Janet Jackson, Sanaa Lathan, Jennifer Lopez, Serena Williams, Vanessa Williams, Terry McMillan, even my sweet baby—the prototype for all Black women—Nia Long, have been publicly scorned by men. And not when they were just some around-the-way broads either. This was when they were already well known and established. I know you're probably thinking, *Why would any man leave these famous, successful, well-established women?* I'll tell you why: men don't care about any of that shit. Men don't care if you have a house, money, career, or trust fund; not an honest man who's just looking for a relationship or wife. You might find some money-hungry men who only want to get at you for the dough, but they're the minority.

One author is a perfect example. She thought she could live her life like one of the characters in her books, and she got a rude awakening. After six years of marriage, her husband told her he was gay. I'm at least glad he admitted he was a fag and didn't use that down-low bullshit. Why would any man in his twenties want to settle down with a broad forty or over? Did she even think before she plunged headfirst into this relationship? That shit simply doesn't happen. It's extremely rare that you'll find a man in his twenties who will settle for a woman in her forties and it's not for sex, money, citizenship, social status, or some other material purpose. When I say extremely rare I'm saying you have a better chance of being eaten by a shark on dry land than for a relationship like this to work. She better wake the fuck up and stop trying to live her life like one of her novels. This world isn't a utopia, bitch, get a clue.

The author thinks, *I've had problems with men all my life. My problems have even given me the material to become a best-selling author. I'm in my forties now, and I have money, status, and a flourishing career, and this young man wants to be with me and I think he's the one.* Yeah, right. Get it together. You know better than that. I know she was probably searching for love and everything but use your heart in combination with common sense. Stay grounded in reality and not fantasy. Anyway, any time a younger man is with a much older woman that shit is a red flag that something is amiss. Young men don't go around looking for old, worn-out broads to bun up with. If nobody your age wants you, what makes you think somebody much younger does?

INVESTING TIME

Do you want a man? You say you want a man, right? How much time do you invest in trying to get one? What do you do other than walk around and go to the club? Are you in shape?

Can you cook? Do you know how to keep a clean house? Do you have an Internet dating profile? Do you know that the average woman spends more time shopping than she does trying to get a man? The average woman spends more time researching shoes and outfits than she does trying to find a man.

Single, heterosexual men, on the other hand, probably spend seventy-five to eighty percent of their time every day in the interest of women. When a man wakes up in the morning, brushes his teeth, showers, and shaves, that's for women. If he was going to only be around other men, he wouldn't care how he looked or smelled. When a man picks out his clothes for the day, that's done for women. He wants to look as attractive as possible to the opposite sex. When a man goes off to school or work, that's done for women. He wouldn't care if he was as dumb as a box of hair and had no money if there weren't any women around. When a man goes to the gym, that's done for women. Why would he care if he had a fat gut if there weren't any women around?

Do you see how much time men put into pursuing women? Anything with any kind of value or substance is going to take hard work, time, and effort to achieve—obtaining a college degree, starting a business, raising a child. The same thing goes for getting a man. It must be at the top of your priority list with the rest of your life goals. It's the most important goal you'll ever aspire to achieve in life. Getting your master's degree, starting a business, or becoming financially free are nothing if you don't have anyone to share it with. On your priority list, getting a man should be above getting your master's, starting a business, becoming more involved in church or getting a promotion at work. You have to ask yourself what you really want in life: a college degree, a business, to be church deacon or a manager at work, or would you prefer more than sixty-five years of marital bliss? The choice is up to you. What is more important to you? If getting a man is not in the top three of your life goals, then you need to ask yourself why. Don't ever put your man last.

2

HOW MEN THINK

You have entered the abyss, the hole through which no light can enter nor escape the mind of a man. Are you ready? Because here it goes. Here are the three things that men want the most: pussy, food, and relaxation. I can't give you every man's exact thoughts. That would be impossible unless I was Professor X of the X-Men, but I can provide you with the basics. The things men want are very simple. The question is whether women want to provide them. Are women willing to provide them? Are women happy to provide them—without hostility? We'll see.

For men, pussy is the foundation from which all else must be formed. Think of pussy as fertile soil. Without it, nothing can grow. A masculine heterosexual man is going to have pussy on the brain 24/7. Let me rewrite that because I don't think you understood me. I said, *a masculine heterosexual man is going to have pussy on the brain 24/7.*

As a woman, can you understand this? Think of something you love. For women, it's probably something like money, shoes, clothes, shopping, or possibly even dick. Well, a man loves pussy a hundred times more than you love any of those things. Pussy is the medication for all of a man's ills. If he's upset, give him some pussy, and he'll calm down. If he's sad, give him some pussy, and that will help alleviate that sadness. If he's tired, a lot of times pussy will give him energy. Pussy first. Everything else is secondary. Can you comprehend this? I doubt it because most women can't. Either they know and don't want to accept it, or they don't want to submit to it.

A heterosexual man is going to weigh these options in his head when on a date, hanging out, or doing almost anything else: pussy, food, and relaxation. Where do you think the phrase, "the best way to a man's heart is through his stomach," came from? It's somewhat true. A female who has learned the proper way to cook has just acquired a very valuable asset. There is a difference between Sara Lee products and homemade. There is a difference between Pillsbury biscuits and homemade ones. Remember that shit when you're in the kitchen and you think you're doing something and you're not doing anything but warming some shit up in the oven. Take some time and study the art of cooking. It will help you out in so many ways in trying to get and keep a man.

Pussy, food, and relaxation. I'm pretty confident you know what pussy and food are, but let me break down relaxation for you. There are three basic parts:

1. **Not talking so much.** A man hates to have to listen to someone talk about nothing. He also hates to be on the phone talking about nothing. When a man calls someone, it's usually for a reason. Women just like to talk—period—and a lot of times they just want a man to listen. Sometimes we don't want to. Many times men just don't feel like talking—at all. Here is a clue that your man doesn't feel like talking: If he doesn't start a conversation with you, then he doesn't feel like talking.

Not thinking so much or zoning out. Men like to zone out—a lot. That means not thinking about the pressures of life or anything. We just want to clear our minds for a while and chill. This is how we get rid of our stress without actually killing somebody. Watching TV, sleeping, relaxing outside on the porch or hammock while having a drink or smoke are a few ways that men zone out. This is why men get so mad when women interrupt these moments. We're trying to relax and here you come with some bullshit like, "We need to talk" or "Did you take out the trash?" or "Do I look fat in this?" Yes, bitch, you look fat. If you have to ask, then yes, damn it, your big ass looks fat in that shit. Now go run some laps and leave me the hell alone; I'm relaxing.

Sleep/Relaxation. This means can a man relax and fall asleep without a woman doing something stupid like rifling through his pockets to see if he has any numbers. Or going through his cell phone and calling numbers or if you're at his house, answering his phone or checking the caller ID to see who calls.

Three simple things—that's all we ask for. Not much, right? If you can accomplish this in combination with you having your physical appearance together, there's no way you won't be able to get a man.

Let's explore a few scenarios so you can better understand what I'm trying to get across.

THE FIRST DATE — SCENARIO I

A man goes on a first date with a female he just met. The average single man usually has more than one chick anyway, and he's always looking to expand. This is one of those opportunities. How the date goes will foretell this new female's category. Before the date, he's thinking about what, ladies? Pussy, that's what. Not the first-date female's pussy because if he's trying to feel her out as wife material, then he doesn't even want to fuck on the first date. But if the opportunity presents itself, then so be it. The odds are not very good that he will fuck on the first date, and he's already prepared for this. Most likely he has an idea of where he might be taking her for the date, so he thinks, *Which broad is closer to her house or the place we're going?* He calls up one of the chicks in his harem and tells her he's hanging out with the fellas and he might be stopping by. Since he's already had sex with this broad and she's used to the routine, she can't wait to get some booty-call dick, so she's all for it. He picks up the female for the first date and they go out and do their thing. During the date, he's thinking, *Is it possible that I could fuck her tonight?* This is just a natural male response.

No matter how Christianized, how holier than thou, or moral you think this man is, believe me, he wants to fuck regardless of your own misguided views. Wanting to have sex and trying to get it are two different things. Don't get them confused. He may want to have sex, but if he's trying to feel you out or is worried that he may offend you, then he won't try. If you're sexy enough, sometimes the urge to try to hit overpowers all. By the way a woman's dressed and how the conversation goes, a man can pretty much tell how the night will turn out.

They have a good date, and he drops her off. She teases him a little with a peck on the lips, and she lets him feel the ass while they hug. The date ends. If she had her appearance in order then he was turned on by her the minute he picked her up and has been for the last four hours or however long the date lasted. Now he needs somewhere to release this sexual tension. No sooner than he drops her off, then he's on the phone with one of his regulars letting her know he's stopping through. He gets to her house and bangs the pussy out, imagining it's the chick he just went out with. Now, could you tell where the pussy, food, and relaxation came in? Pussy preparation was taken care of before the date even started. Food was handled during the date, and pussy and relaxation came after the date.

THE FAKE CHRISTIAN OCCULTIST OR BASIC HOLDOUT — SCENARIO II

Before I begin, ladies, here's a little info. Men don't care if you hold off from having sex. It's not going to make us respect you any more. As a matter of fact, it's a thin line between holding out so we won't think you're a freak and holding out too long. When you hold out too long, all it does is piss us off. When you withhold sex from a man for no reason other than you think he should wait for it longer, he slowly starts to withdraw the feelings and respect he has for you. As soon as he gets the pussy, he's just going to treat you like shit for holding out for nothing. I mean think about it, how much shit can you talk about? It gets to the point where you've covered everything, and there's nothing else to do but fuck. The average person's life is not that complicated. If you sat and just listened to someone talk about their life, they could pretty much cover everything within an hour. Once it gets to this point and a woman keeps holding out, it becomes boring and men lose interest—fast. A man is still going to want to hit because he's invested all that time. Remember this important fact, too, ladies. If you say to your man, "Don't even try it because you ain't getting none tonight." That might be true. He may not be getting any from *you*, but if he's a seasoned veteran he's getting some from another female.

So let's get to the scenario.

A man goes out on a date with a so-called Christian broad. This is like their tenth date, and he still hasn't gotten anywhere, and he's getting bored real fast. After about the fifth unproductive date, all a man hears is *blah, blah, blah* anyway. He doesn't even care what she's saying but he has to sit through it and listen if he wants to get anywhere with her. Since he knows he's not going to fuck from jump street, he's either already had sex before he came to pick her up or he has it set up for afterward. Food will be taken care of during the date, and relaxation is always available since there isn't any sex going on. The date will be quick and cheap. There's no need to wine and dine for no pussy. The date ends, and he drops her off to go fuck some other chick. The next time the Christian broad calls, he's going to be cautious about going out with her. A date with a definite "No Pussy" tag attached to it is always going to be on a man's terms.

The Christian broad calls and tells him how she's had such a nice time going out with him the past few months and she would like to take the relationship to the next level. She wants a more intimate setting so the potential to hit just gained a few points. She cooks him dinner. He goes over her house and they do the romantic candlelight dinner thing and then she lets him fuck. Afterward he realizes that it wasn't even that good. Big mistake. She made him wait and the sex wasn't even good. From this point on, he will no longer go out with her because he wants to recoup the money he spent on dates in pussy payments. He's now at an advantage. He's withdrawn the feelings he had for her over the time she had him waiting for no reason. She's caught feelings for him but the sex was whack. In the process of holding out for nothing, she's turned him off completely. All he will do now is give her the runaround about committing to a long-term relationship. Or he'll lie to get more sex until she gets tired of it. He will still keep her around as long as possible because pussy that's not that good is better than no pussy at all.

Now tell me what was the point of holding out? All she did in this scenario was get caught up in a position to be hurt. Don't get yourself trapped in the pussy game with a man because you can't win. It's like going to Vegas and trying to beat the house. How can you beat the house when the odds are purposely stacked against you? You might slip up and win on occasion, but in the long run, that ass is his—literally.

THE VETERAN FEMALE — SCENARIO III

A man meets a woman at some random place and gets her number. He calls her, and they arrange a date. Pussy preparation is thought about immediately, and the usual plans are set in motion. He picks her up, and she's dressed in a very provocative outfit. The potential for pussy on this date just gained a few points because she has on her come-fuck-me outfit. When she gets in the car, she smells just as good as she looks.

During the date, she's made sure to be overly touchy-feely. It's a nice date, and they head back home. During the ride he asks, if she would like to come back to his place for some drinks. She accepts, and they proceed to his house. They grab some drinks, do a little talking, and he makes a few moves on her. She doesn't stop him, and they proceed to the bedroom. The sex is hot and passionate. She's loud but restrained, kinky but subdued. After sex, he either drops her back at her house or lets her spend the night. If the sex was good, then she's definitely spending the night, regardless of how early he has to get up. If he drops her at her house, it doesn't mean the sex wasn't good—she might have something to do the next morning. Either way he is going to be able to sleep and relax if she's there or not. He tells her he'll call.

The man now has a few choices here. He can:

- Treat this as only a one-night stand and never call her again.
- Add her to the roster.
- Disregard that she let him fuck on the first date and keep on seeing her seriously in hopes of beginning a long-term relationship. I would say it's about a fifty-fifty chance of men starting a relationship with a one-night stand so the odds are pretty good.

Do you see how easy it would be for a man to fall for the third scenario every time? He accomplished pussy, food, and relaxation without any complications, and he didn't even have to share his bed. Believe me, if the pussy was good, this broad is getting a call the next day. Just because you have sex on the first date doesn't make you a whore. There are plenty of people who are now married who had sex with each other on the first date. If the chemistry is there, then why fight it? *Love Jones*, one of my favorite movies, typifies this point. Sometimes you need to let your heart lead the way and not your mind.

Think of pussy as being a highly addictive drug, such as heroin, for all heterosexual men, and women are the suppliers. If a man has a habitual drug habit—drugs, meaning pussy—then can you imagine the lengths a man would take in order to keep it in full supply? He would have several different suppliers (in different locations) with different grades of product (quality of pussy). If he knows supplier A in location B has the best product, then supplier A is going to get first choice every time. If supplier A is unavailable, then a man is going to think, *Okay, product B is too dry, C is not freaky enough, D cums too quick, E has too much hair, F talks too much, and G acts crazy.* From A to Z he is going to weigh his options. Then he is going to make an informed decision on whom to call.

Ladies, let's reverse the situation and place men in the same scenarios. Which man would you call?

3

BLACK MEN ARE INTIMIDATED BY ATTRACTIVE, SUCCESSFUL, EDUCATED SISTAS

This is a complete and total myth that has been perpetrated by women who can't seem to get or keep a man. Don't be mad because men don't want you. There is a reason why you're alone, and that reason is you. It's not men, it's not the brothers, society, your schedule, your job, your income, your religion, your professional or social status; it's you. You're the cause of yourself being single. What women have to realize is that they are the only constant in these failed relationships. The men change as women go from one relationship to another. If all these relationships are failing, I think it's foolish to blame everyone else or label every man as a dog, intimidated, or inferior without looking at the one thing that remains constant, which is yourself. If a female went to ten different psychiatrists and all of them labeled her clinically insane, would you think the female was sane and the psychiatrists were wrong? The female is the only thing that remains constant.

What man with any kind of sophistication or values is intimidated by a woman? Why do women think this way? Because you may have a better job than him, do you think he's intimidated by you? Maybe it's because you're more educated than he is. Could it be that you make more money or you're taller? Yeah, that's it, that's why you're alone because you have all these things and he doesn't. He's jealous of you and of your success. Bitch, please. This is what you tell yourself to help your self-esteem and to justify that you're alone.

You're alone because you've forgotten the fact that you're a woman. You're out of touch with your feminine side. No masculine heterosexual man wants a woman who acts like a man. For the most part, sistas are smart-mouthed, pushy, overbearing, overweight, and overly critical, have become obsessively involved in church and the lives of their children or friends, and are basically clueless about men. This is in part because Black culture or society, in general, has taught women that a man should find *you*. Society has taught Black women to falsely believe that they're queens, they should sit perched upon pedestals, and all available successful men should chase after them. In the words of comedian Paul Mooney, "Wake up, nigga. Wake up." Women think they can sit around, and their soul mate will just come knocking at the front door. This type of woman has probably done nothing her entire life to attract a man.

Having a good job, house, car, business, or education does nothing to attract a man. These are things men do to attract women. These things are icing on the cake. If the cake itself is horrible, no amount of icing will make it taste better. If a man could have sex with you on some oil-stained clothes behind a Dumpster, he would. Men try to obtain things like an education, house, nice car, or business to attract women because we know women like these things. It gives women the impression that a man is stable, secure, established, and a good provider. Other than that, men wouldn't do any of that shit if women didn't like it. But women haven't done the same for men.

If you want a man, then what have you done or what are you

doing to attract one? If you want a man, then you have to try to obtain the things that men want, which are an attractive appearance; being open-minded sexually; not running your yap twenty-four hours a day; learning how to cook, clean, and how to be a good mother; becoming more interested in the things we enjoy like sporting events, cars, and motorcycles. These are some of the things that men want—simple and plain. Even learning how to cook, clean, being a good mother, and trying to learn about the things we like is optional if you have the first three in order.

Men are natural hunters, so we go out of our way to find out where the attractive women are, what they like, and the best way to get one. That means participating in activities we really don't enjoy just to please women. How many heterosexual men do you think you'd find at an opera or ballet if their women didn't drag them along? Men don't particularly like these things, but we know some women enjoy them, so we'll sit through it, grin and bear it to appease them.

How many times have you sat through a football or basketball game without asking a bunch of questions, and just cheered when he cheered and got upset when he got upset? It's not that hard. If the blue team scores, and he cheers, you cheer. If the white team scores and he boos, you boo. You don't have to know what's going on. You're just there to support him. If you don't understand the game, then get a book, DVD or whatever and learn the rules on your own time. Doing something like this will impress him more than asking a bunch of questions before, during, and after the game he's trying to watch.

Unless a man knows fluent Italian, then he doesn't know what the fuck is being said at an opera. But he will sit through it and watch your emotions. And when you clap, he claps; when you cry, he comforts you. You should be trying to do the same for your would-be man. If you see that the team your man is rooting for has lost, then you don't have to say much—maybe something like, "That was bullshit." Then ask him if he wants something to eat or drink and walk away. When he calms down, believe me he'll come find you. Most men will be a little agitated if their team lost so don't run your mouth saying stupid shit like, "Aw, poor baby. Did your team lose again?" That's just cause for an instant ass whipping. You see, for men, watching sports is another way we get to release testosterone and frustration just like women get an emotional release by watching the events they enjoy.

TRADING LOW ON THE STOCK MARKET OF RELATIONSHIPS

I need to make it clear that after age thirty you're no longer looked upon the same by men. In other words, at age twenty-three, if you were a stock and trading at twenty-three dollars a share, by the time you reach age thirty the stock price is at $2.50 and falling fast. I mention this because a lot of women believe they can get their education, business, or career first, then worry about getting a man. This is not the case. Women have a very short window to secure a lasting relationship. I would say ten to twelve years from ages eighteen to age thirty, give or take a few years.

After age thirty, the odds of a woman finding a man who has the qualities she desires drops dramatically. This is somewhat in part to childbearing. If a man is looking to start a family, doing so with a female who's thirty or older is not as easy as it would be with one who's twenty-six whose body is younger and can rebound faster. Her eggs are younger, and the child has the likelihood of being born healthy and free from any complications.

This is not something that men got together one day and came up with; this is natural male instinct. A man is going to naturally gravitate toward a younger female if he's looking to start a family. If a woman is well established in her career and financially secure but is over thirty, a man will likely settle down with someone younger who has potential if he's looking to start a family.

4

TAKING ADVICE FROM SINGLE WOMEN

I encountered this subject daily while doing research for this book. Every time I'd talk to a female about what course of action she takes to acquire a man, about her relationships with men, or what she did when the relationship hit a trouble spot, I'd hear things like, "Well, I talked to my girls about it, and they told me to do XYZ" or "I told my mother we were having trouble, and she told me to do so and so." I'd just shake my head.

As a single woman in the United States or wherever you're residing, why in the world would you take advice on how to get a man from another single woman? She's alone. What is she going to do, give you advice on how to be alone? Would you take advice from a bum on how to make money? Would you go to a dentist who has bad teeth? What about going to an obese personal trainer? Chris Farley did a sketch about an obese personal trainer on *Saturday Night Live*, and it was funny as hell, but I digress.

Anyway if you wouldn't do any of these things then why would you take advice from a single woman with no man on how to get or please a man? Single women don't know shit about how to get a man. That's why they're single. Most married women don't know either because they will lie to you about how they came to be married. They'll likely tell stories, embellishing the truth on how they met a boy and molded him into a man. Bullshit.

The only single women who know anything about how to get or please a man are prostitutes. They deal with men twenty-four hours a day, seven days a week. They have to because their livelihood depends on it. Prostitutes know more about getting and keeping a man than any woman you know. Five years as a streetwalking prostitute is the equivalent of a highly qualified sex therapist with a Ph.D. If you're bold enough, make a night of it. Ask a man or one of your girlfriends if they know any upscale prostitutes. Don't get some ninety-eight-pound crackhead who you've seen scurrying around in your neighborhood. I'm talking about a phat-ass, big-titty, undisputed, bona-fide bottom bitch. Pay her for her services and have your questions ready. Ask her about her techniques on sex and how to please a man. Ask her if she had a man, how she would go about keeping him interested all the time. Ask her how she treats her man. Ask her what she would do if she spotted a man she was interested in. I bet you her advice will be well worth the money—better than Dr. Ruth, Mother Love, Oprah, or any other dried-up scallywag trying to give sex advice any day.

Don't want to ask a prostitute? Then if you want advice on how to get or please a man, ask a single man. I can't stress this enough. When I say ask a single man, I don't mean your gay friend, either. Also don't ask your overweight neighbor Stanley who you've never seen with a human woman before and who you think might be sniffing ladies' underwear in the community washroom. Don't even ask a married male friend or your married girlfriend. Ask a sexually active single heterosexual man.

The reason why you don't want to ask a married man is because most of the time if he's married, then he's been out of the game too long. The extent of his dating knowledge will end on the date he was married if he's faithful to his wife. If he's not faithful then he's still out there and you can go to him for answers. A married man is like a solitary male lion in the wild who is trying to gain control over a pride of female lions. As a solitary male he has to struggle and fight to gain control of the pride. He has to prove to the pride that he can lead. And lastly he has to defeat the older male lion who is currently in charge. But once he achieves his goal of gaining control of the pride, the lion relaxes, and his priorities change from gaining control of the pride to defending it.

This is the married man, the relaxed and content male lion. As a single, sexually active heterosexual man, you must stay on top of the game because the players change but the game remains the same. I know that's kind of hard to understand, but single men know what I mean when I say that. Sexually active, single, heterosexual men, for the most part, must always be on top of their game. They have to be if they want any pussy. And that's basically what the game for men is about—getting pussy. You might find that vulgar or crass but hey, that's life. I'm giving you the truth straight from a man's perspective. If you want to beat around the bush or have your information sugarcoated, then pick up another damn book because this one ain't for you. That's what dating is all about. That's why men put up with some females' smart mouths and bad attitudes—to eventually get the ass. It's that simple. That's what we need, and you have it. There's a phrase some men use: "Ain't no pussy like new pussy." This is pretty much self-explanatory: even if you have something good in-house, it's still not as good as something new.

By the way if you ever run into a man who tells you all pussy is the same, then don't listen to another word that stupid muthafucka has to say because either he's lying about how much experience he has with women or he's just a plain old idiot. All pussy is different. Every single piece of ass I've ever had has been different, and believe me I've had plenty. That's why men chase women all the time; because it's all different. If it was the same, then the first girl a man fucked he'd marry and that would be the end of it.

Back to what I was saying...the game is about getting pussy, and if you can comprehend this concept, then you can control the situation, i.e. control the game. If you understand the fact that as a woman you have the pussy and that's the *only* reason why some men deal with you, then you can control the game. That might be hard to hear, but hey, life is hard. Deal with it. If you can set aside your emotions for a second and understand what I'm trying to tell you, then you can control who you give the pussy to and not fall for the okey-doke. Some men will say or do anything just to get a piece of ass. Women often fall for the same bullshit-ass lines over and over. As a woman, you have to pick and choose who you give the pussy to and be very selective about it. You should be able to look back at the relationships that you've had with men that didn't work out for one reason or another and not be disgusted with yourself for sleeping with any of them.

When and if I ever have a daughter, I'm going to school her the same way. I'm going to try my best to give her the information about the world and the relationships between men and women as straight as possible without hurting her feelings. I will make her understand that you can be the girlfriend of the star quarterback on the high school football team, but you don't have to fuck him to do so. I will tell her not to judge a man by his material possessions. Just because he has a nice job, house, and car doesn't make him any more of a man.

Judge him by the man he is, not because of what he has. Watch his actions. Judge him with the same scrutiny you would a man with an average job and small bank account who lives in an apartment. If ever there is a time that my would-be daughter would bring a man into the house that she is interested in marrying, I would grill him the same way if he was a doctor, lawyer, dentist, football star, hip-hop artist, UPS driver, or government worker. I would want to know how much he loved and cared for her and how he plans to treat her, not what he can provide for her. Material items can be taken away instantly but love—real love—lasts forever. People say love doesn't last forever. I think this is incorrect. True love *does* last forever. Think about it. When a loved one passes away, years after they've been gone, the love you have for them never fades. It's always there.

I'm not talking about that love where you go out with a female and two years later y'all are still dating and she tells you that she wants to get married or she can't date you anymore. You propose like a dummy just because you're comfortable with her and have been with her for so long. Not that bullshit. I'm talking about when you're ten years old and you get that first kiss while playing house in the backyard. Years later when you're thirteen and the school bully is picking on her you stand in and potentially take an ass whipping to protect her. You earn the bully's respect and hers for being her brave warrior. At sixteen you're both virgins. She calls you over to her house because her parents are out of town and you sneak upstairs to her room, being careful not to wake her little brother, and have that first sexual experience. Her parents come home early and you have to jump your half-naked ass out her second-floor bedroom window and high-tail it down the street because you know if her father catches you, he will lynch your little ass. But they never find out.

At age eighteen you both go to different colleges and lose contact. You date other people, but it's not the same. At age twenty-four you're finally out of school with a master's degree and you've started that business you've always wanted but something is missing. At age twenty-five you run into her while visiting your mother. You talk briefly and discuss old times. Amazingly she's still single and available. Maybe she's been waiting for someone. She gives you her number, and before long you've hooked back up and it feels so good to be with her again. She fits perfectly into your life, like a piece to a puzzle. Every time you kiss her, it reminds you of the first time. Within a year you're married. Every morning when you leave the house without her, you can't wait to get home. One evening when you get home you come into the house and she doesn't know you're there. You walk through the house to where she is. She has her back turned to you, and she doesn't see you. She's making dinner for you, and it's your favorite. You don't disturb her. She's wearing a necklace that you bought her in high school. You can't believe she still has it. You smile and quietly laugh to yourself because it reminds you of the time you bought it for her. You both skipped school on her birthday to spend the whole day together. It took you the entire summer to buy it but you did. You still remember the look on her face when you gave it to her. You realize without her, there is no you. It scares you to think about what would become of you if something were to happen to her. You start to tear up. Just before the tear drops she turns around, startled. You run to her and pick her up. You spin her around and hug her tight. You kiss her passionately, and she makes that little moan you like. You put her down and look into her eyes. Without saying a word she damn near cries from the emotion she sees in your eyes. It's like through both your eyes the energy of the love you have for each other is being transferred back and forth. You give her a peck on the lips, tell her you love her, and you let her get back to cooking. Hell yeah! That's the type of love I'm talking about. That kind of love never fades.

Boy, just writing that brought back some memories. Damn, I wish I could go back. Go back to stealing pieces of my grandmother's fried corn bread off the kitchen counter, talking all night on the phone. "You hang up." "No, you hang up." Man, what I would do to relive those moments again knowing what I know now. But anyway, I'm way off the subject. Let me just end this paragraph right now before I start writing about when Jodeci and *Diary of a Mad Band* came out and how this chick that I used to mess with had so many good times listening to it. Well, I wouldn't exactly call it listening, if you know what I mean.

5

MEN ON THE "DOWN LOW"

I've had numerous discussions about this particular situation. I've come to one conclusion about men on the down low. There is no DL. These muthafuckas are just plain gay. I don't even like to use the term *DL*, but I will for the sake of this chapter. So-called DL men have actually stolen a heterosexual term and perverted it. The term used to define keeping something secret from one's wife or girlfriend. When a man would be with his mistress, a man would say something like, "Let's keep this on the down low," meaning let's keep this between us. Two men fucking had nothing to do with the original meaning of down low.

The reason why I've come to the conclusion men on the DL are gay is that as a heterosexual male I cannot foresee a time when I will want to get out of bed with a chick and get poked in the ass by a dude or poke a dude in the ass. I'm just not seeing a connection with that. So I think to myself. I say, *Self, who does want to have anal sex with men? Oh I know, gay men.* I know it's going to be a lot of females who read this and say, "Oh no, honey, DL men are out there, and I know some." No, sweetheart, you know some gay men. You know some gay men who are in deep, deep denial. That's what I call DL, the "Denial Lifestyle."

I watched the same *Oprah* show when the author of the book who so-called exposed the DL phenomenon was on there talking about it. The females in the audience were hanging on to his every word. Even his daughter came on talking about how she didn't know. Please. That nigga was gay. Talking like he had marbles in his mouth. I have no idea why his voice sounded the way it did, but it probably comes from all the dicks he's sucked. Anyway, let me explain my reasoning on this matter. Being gay or on the DL is not a sexual thing. A lot of people will find this hard to believe or can't accept it. A lot of these same people probably don't know that homosexuality was previously diagnosed as a mental disorder. Only in 1973 did the American Psychiatric Association change its stance on this issue.

According to the *Harvard Salient*, in 1973 the American Psychiatric Association (APA) came to no longer regard homosexual attractions as a psychological disorder, and instead decided that these attractions can only be considered a mental disorder if they caused the individual "distress and social disability."

The major reason they reclassified homosexuality as a mental disorder is because of rioting and threats from gay rights groups, not because of actual scientific research. Even to this very day, the debate has been given new life because of the gay marriage issue. Now there's a new twist. Doctors are saying with reparative therapy a gay person can become straight. Be well informed before you jump on the DL bandwagon. If you sit back and think about it, from my point of view, it makes perfect sense that homosexuality, or men on the DL, would be a mental disorder because number one, a high percentage of homosexuals were sexually abused as children, which in turn had an effect on them choosing an alternative lifestyle. Females have an ass also. But these particular men don't want a female; they want some ashy, hairy-knuckled dude to have sex with. A woman can perform the same sexual acts that a man can. A woman can even use a strap-on if she so chooses, but the fact still remains that these men don't want a woman. They want a man, which means they are not on the DL—they're gay.

By the way, if your man ever asks you to use a strap-on while you're with him, then that's a big red flag that he could have fag potential. I wouldn't go so far as to call him a homosexual because the act is still with a woman, but the possibility is definitely there. If a man wants to get poked in the ass by a stiff, hard object, then you need to fully recognize that something may be more than a little wrong, ya dig? I would think a woman who is concerned that her man might be on the DL would notice certain signs about him.

Before I get into this, let me state that there are no signs for heterosexual men. What I mean by this is a heterosexual man is not going to display homosexual signs. You're never going to catch a heterosexual man slipping up and saying something like, "Oh, he's sexy" or "I wish I had arms like his." These are things gay men say. If your man is exhibiting any kind of signs, this means he's gay, bisexual, on the DL, or has potential to be gay, that's it, and that's all. Don't overlook obvious signs because you're feeling him and you want it to work. Don't say to yourself, *I didn't just hear that, did I?* Or you catch him staring at a dude and you say to yourself, *Well, maybe they know each other.* Don't do this dumb shit. If he's a fag then he's a fag, and there's nothing as a woman you can do to change that. He has to want to change that shit for himself.

I repeat, a heterosexual man is not going to exhibit any signs. If he's straight then he's straight and he has pussy on the brain 24/7. There is no room for gay shit in there. Don't get me wrong now. There are some men who are more effeminate than others, but they still will only go so far if they're heterosexual. As for the signs, I think a very good one that your man has potential or is gay, on the DL, whatever, is if he looks other men in the eye while not speaking to them.

This was also discussed by the author of the *Down Low* book while on *Oprah*. He stated, "No words have to be spoken; I can make a connection with another man just by looking him in the eye." Ladies, straight men don't look other straight men in the eyes unless we are speaking or making some sort of silent gesture of communication. No straight man is going to walk down the street looking other dudes in the face. Number one, it's gay; and number two, it's a waste of time and energy. Why look other dudes in the face when we can watch phat-ass bitches walk by while our women aren't looking? Single heterosexual men will look damn near every attractive female in the face for some sort of eye contact. Heterosexual men take eye contact from a female as a sign that she's interested. Can you imagine you're walking with your man and another man walks by and they stare each other in the eyes—not glance, stare—and they don't say anything? That shit is gay right there. Ladies, just sit back and watch your man one day. If you know he's straight and you're walking or driving with him and another dude looks him in the eyes too long and doesn't say anything, his first reaction would be to say to you something like, "What the fuck is he looking at?" or something along this line. He's not going to be okay with it and just smile. If he does, then there's your sign that something isn't right. And you should run for the border, or better yet, run your cute ass over to my house—only if you're sexy and in shape, of course. Bring your HIV/STD test results with you, and I'll definitely handle that business for you.

6

THERE'S NO SUCH THING AS SINGLE AND FABULOUS

Stop faking that you're happy being alone. The worst lie you can tell is a lie to yourself. Even if you're young, rich, and successful, you still don't want to be alone. You want someone to share it with. The government of the United States didn't come up with the type of jailing system that we currently have today for nothing. They know that a lifetime alone is torture. That's why the worst criminals get locked away for years in solitary confinement. It's one of the worst forms of psychological torture. Being without human contact affects the mind and changes it permanently.

An example of this was in the movie *Castaway*. Tom Hanks became attached to this soccer ball, which was his only companion for years on a deserted island—he risked his life to retrieve it when it washed away. Since he couldn't save the original ball, when he was finally rescued, he purchased another one because all of the years of being alone on that island had created an everlasting bond with this ball that was permanently etched in his brain. Again I reflect on Maslow's hierarchy of needs.

Love/Belonging needs

After physiological and safety needs are fulfilled, the third layer of human needs is social. This involves emotionally based relationships in general, such as friendship, sexual-relationship, or having a family. Humans want to be accepted, and to belong to groups, whether it be clubs, work groups, religious groups, family, gangs, etc. They need to feel loved (sexually and non-sexually) by others, and to be accepted by them. People also have a constant desire to feel needed. In the absence of these elements, people become increasingly susceptible to loneliness, social anxieties, and depression.

The need for love and affection has to be fulfilled in some form or fashion. If not you become deficient, and situations such as transferring those feelings to an inanimate object like a soccer ball occur.

WHERE I AM, HE SHOULD BE, TOO

For a lot of women I've spoken with, they feel if a man is not at a certain point in life by the time a woman is then he's not datable. If you get your undergraduate degree at twenty-two and your master's at twenty-four, what makes you think a man should have the same thing at the same time you do? Life happens. Some people have it easier than others. If you went straight through school without having a job and any financial difficulties, then that means you probably had a strong family backing. A lot of people don't have that. They have to make do on their own. They may not have even wanted to pursue their master's or bachelor's degree. To isolate yourself to men who only have college degrees leaves you in a very shallow pool. Don't resign yourself to such things. Sometimes you have to go three steps back to take one step forward.

7

ARE YOU AN INDIRECT PROSTITUTE?

The dictionary defines a prostitute as "*one who engages in sexual activity indiscriminately, especially for money.*" When a man and a woman first meet, you both know what it's all about. Ultimately you both want to have sex but you have to play the game first, right? During this process, on average, the man is usually footing the bill. Not because he wants to but because this is what's required and accepted by society as the correct practice of courtship. Rarely does the woman pay anything because this is what society has taught women to do.

Usually it starts out slow. A woman meets a man at some random spot, and she feels comfortable enough to give him her number. Soon he calls her, and they talk on and off for a few days until they both arrange a date to meet and go out. He drives over her house to pick her up. He's using his gas (gas money), he takes her out to the movies or wherever (movie money), he takes her out to eat (food money), and then drops her off back home (gas money). Let's add this up, shall we? Around twenty dollars for gas depending upon how far she lives from him, twenty dollars for the movie, and thirty-five dollars for dinner and a tip. Because you know we ain't taking your ass nowhere but to Applebee's for the first date. That comes out to about seventy-five dollars.

This process goes on in different variations and locations until they ultimately have sex. The woman usually hasn't paid a dime throughout this entire process. The only difference between this and a street-walking prostitute is that the street walker eliminates the dinners and movies and just takes the money. You can get a good fuck from a second-rate prostitute on the street for around seventy-five dollars. Some will give you a suck and a fuck for that much. So by this definition, a virgin is the biggest indirect prostitute of all because she requires the largest investment in order to have sex. So when Mommy tells you to go out and get a man who has money and can take care of you, all she's doing is telling you to go out and be the biggest whore you can be. In other words, make him pay for the pussy.

According to the dictionary, that's how a whore is defined. The reason why men who sleep with a lot of women are defined as gigolos, players, and casanovas and not prostitutes is because men will sleep with you for free. They don't care about what you have or what you can get for them. They're just in it strictly for the sex. Stop being so materialistic and judging men by what they have and what they can provide. This is a westernized philosophy of life. African-American women have been unknowingly assimilated hook, line, and sinker into this philosophy. The total disregard to try to recapture a culture that's been lost is overwhelmingly evident in today's current relationships between African-American men and women. In previous years, the woman was happy just being a woman. Just doing her part was reward enough. Now women want to do a man's job also. Everyone can't be the boss. You can't have two presidents. Someone has to lead, and someone has to follow.

Here's a good way to tell who's in charge of the house and who makes the decisions. It's three in the morning. You're awakened by some loud noise. It sounded a lot like the downstairs window breaking. You hear noise from the broken glass crackling under feet as if someone is stepping inside the house. If you get up and go downstairs with a bat or gun and check it out, then you're in charge and you make the decisions. If you have to roll over, wake someone up, tell them what you've heard and ask them to go downstairs and check it out because you're about to piss on yourself, then you don't make any decisions. Even if you own the house financially you're not in charge of it because the person who goes downstairs is the one who's in control. This person wears the pants and is in charge of the relationship and decision-making.

~~CHILD~~ MOTHER SUPPORT

Let's get something straight from the beginning: Child support is a corrupt, biased law for women, just as child rape, sodomy, and molestation are biased laws when it comes to women. That's right, I said it. If a man has sex with an underage girl, the law will try to give him life in prison, register him as a sex offender for the rest of his life, and even try to chemically castrate him. If a woman has sex with an underage boy, the law gives her a slap on the wrist, maybe some community service, and tells her "Just don't do it again." I say clitorally castrate that bitch! I want to see that broad chemically, clitorally castrated on national TV. You want equality, that's some equality for ya ass. If the law is supposed to be just, then it should be just for everyone. It shouldn't be more lenient on women and harsher on men for the same crime.

When it comes to child support, one parent is supposed to pay half of the support for the child and the other parent pays half.

It shouldn't be that whichever parent makes the most money should pay one hundred percent of the support for the child and also pay half, if not all, the support for the other parent. If you can't provide a roof over the head of your child without help, then your qualifications as a parent are in question from the beginning. There are plenty of good men who would love to keep their child full time but they aren't given the option to do so.

The phrase *child support* should be changed to *mother support* because that's who the money is supporting. This is another way the government has turned women into indirect prostitutes. "Mother support" by definition is forced governmental prostitution because we both know, in the majority of cases, that the money isn't being used to support the child. Just because a man had sex with a woman and a child was born and the man is no longer interested in the woman or vice versa, he shouldn't have to support her for the next eighteen years. Because he is no longer interested in continuing a relationship with her for whatever reason, she becomes bitter and wants him to pay her for the sex. If that's not a whore, then what is?

Don't use the bullshit phrase, "The money isn't for me; it's to support our child." Yeah, right. Then why isn't the money required to go directly toward the child's needs? For instance, if the child requires day care, then the money should go directly to the provider. If the child is in private school, then the money should go directly to the school. If the child needs clothes, then gift cards should be given in the child's name or some kind of government card should be created that can be used only for clothing just as the government food stamp card can only be used for food. Receipts of all items purchased should be sent to the father through child support enforcement so he can see exactly where his money is being spent. The mother or custodial parent should never receive *any* cash money. This way the mother of the child can't manipulate the system as is the current state of affairs. Some women will say, what about the mortgage or rent? What about the gas, water, and electric bill? I respond by saying, if you can't afford to pay your own mortgage, rent, water, electric, or gas bill without assistance, then you shouldn't have custody of the child to begin with.

Custodial custody of the child should automatically be deferred to the other party if it's shown that you're not competent and independent enough to take care of yourself without someone else paying sixty percent of your expenses. You're essentially living off that other person. If I were the judge, someone who was paying sixty percent of someone else's expenses and also taking care of him or herself without any other outside assistance, would show me that they need to be the primary caregiver. There should also be a national cap on the amount that can be spent monthly, and it shouldn't be exclusively based on the individual's income. The cap should also be reasonable—for instance, no more than three hundred dollars a month for any one child. I don't see how the government will give you $250 a month for welfare and tell you it's enough for you to take care of a child but will charge the father of a child $850 and the mother can still claim it's not enough. The custodial parent should not be able to live off child support. That is ridiculous.

If you ever find yourself in that type of situation, listen to what questions the judge asks the father. Usually the first question is something like, "Have you been making your child support payments?" "Are all of your child support payments up to date?" "Are you in arrears on any child support?" Notice he won't ask,

"How often does the mother make time for you to see your child?" "When is the last time you saw the child?" "Do you make it a priority to spend quality time with the child?" "Do you consider yourself to be a good parent?" He may ask something like, "How often do you see the child?" or "How often does the child spend the night over your house?" The last statement is just in conjunction with child support so they can calculate how much to charge you. If it's supposed to be a fifty-fifty situation to take care of a child, then why does child support enforcement charge the non-custodial parent with sixty percent of the support? Smells like bullshit to me.

Don't ever make your child's father pay child support if:

- He's doing all he can for the child.
- You know you really don't need the money.
- You're bitter that he's with someone else and not with you.
- Something is still there and you want to try to work it out.
- You want what's best for the child.

Children suffer when women try to pigeonhole the father into paying child support. According to the state, the father doesn't even have to see the child. The state considers him to be an acceptable father because his financial obligation is fulfilled. This is society's new measuring stick on who's considered to be a good father. All they want to know is if a man is paying his child support. If he is, then in the eyes of the law, the government, and some women, he's considered to be a good father. This creates yet another stumbling block for African-American fathers to be in their child's lives. A lot of females are fine with the current corrupt child support system as long as they are getting paid. In the long run, it's the child who suffers.

The tax situation, when it comes to mother support, is ass backward. If a man is paying mother support at the end of the year, all the money that is taken from his check to support the mother is looked at by the government as money he spent on himself. He cannot claim this missing income on his taxes. In turn, in some situations the mother is not required to report the support she's receiving so it's like she's getting the money from him tax free.

Child support is not like a bill where you can rob Peter to pay Paul, as my mother would say. It is an ongoing eighteen-year debt that a man must continue paying whether he's unemployed, ill, locked up, or whatever. It's a ridiculous law that needs to be abolished or restructured for the changing times. Only in cases where the parent of the child is totally ignoring his or her financial and moral responsibilities toward the child should support be enforced.

BUY ME A DRINK

Why? Why don't I just give you the ten dollars. Are you out of your fucking mind? For the record, I don't buy drinks for females. Let me explain this. If I'm in the club, lounge, bar, or wherever liquor is served, and I'm having a conversation with a female and we start to hit if off, if I decide that I want another drink I may ask if she wants anything also. But to buy some random trollop a drink out the blue—never. For what? What's my motivation? Some women even call men cheap or broke for not buying them a drink. I could never understand this logic. How is a woman going to call a man cheap when she is the one who is asking *him* to buy *her* a drink? Obviously he has money and she doesn't.

Some women just go out to see how many drinks they can get random men to buy. This is in some way how they gauge their attractiveness to the opposite sex. Explain to me how this isn't prostitution? Anytime you're accepting money or gifts from someone in exchange for something that has a sexual connotation to it, it's prostitution. They arrest men and women for this very thing every day. If an undercover female officer walks down the street and says to any random man, "Hey, baby, you want a date?" The man then asks, "How much?" The officer states, "Fifty bucks." The man inquires, "What do I get for fifty bucks?" The officer says, "Everything." If the man then says, "Okay, let's go," this is when he can be arrested for engaging prostitution.

Tell me how this is different from a female walking up to a man in a club and asking him to buy her a drink. The man is only buying the drink because he has a preconceived notion that if he buys it, maybe he will be able to talk to the female and have sex with her. This is the same as with the man who is approached by the officer. The man has the preconceived notion he will be able to have sex with this woman if he pays the fifty dollars.

Do you know how many dumb muthafuckas I see buying drinks for these gold-digging, dirt-rat skanks? It's too many to mention. These are the type of women who get fucked and never get called again and wonder why they have four kids by different fathers and no man. I'm going to say this for me because I don't know if the majority of men may think this way. For me if a female walks up to me and asks me to buy her a drink, I find it rude and offensive. I also think she looks at me to be some sort of sucker. These are the females who get used repeatedly for sex and they're thrown away like worn-out gym socks. I've seen females go up to men and ask them for a drink, he buys it, and she doesn't give him any play. She walks away and goes to sit with her girls or something. Then she'll come back and ask the same sucker for another drink, this time for her and one of her friends. He buys the drinks, she still doesn't give him any play, and walks away. What kind of shit is this? Or should I ask what kind of clown is he? This whack individual is what starts women thinking they can do this to every man.

All women who want men to spend money on them or who are making money in conjunction with providing sexual favors are prostitutes, be it directly or indirectly. Even if there is no physical contact but just the slightest indication of anything of a sexual nature, you are still an indirect prostitute. Strippers, video hoes, lingerie models, bikini-clad models, it's basically in the same category as soft-core porn. Don't fool yourself.

The amount of money you spend on someone has nothing to do with how much you like and care for them. Men view any financial investment in a woman as a potential pussy payment. Stop whoring yourself out indirectly. This behavior will be passed down to your daughters. Children imitate what they see. Once a little girl sees Mommy hugged up under some man after he's taken her out to dinner, she will do the same thing at school when it's lunchtime with some random boy who is inclined to buy her lunch. Now she just gave up that fifteen-year-old virgin pussy for a $1.75 school lunch. As she matures, the price may increase, but her behavior will remain the same.

8

RELATIONSHIP LIES AND RELIGION

This is the chapter for all you Bible-humping women out there. I feel it's my duty as a man to enlighten these brainwashed, westernized, Bible-toting, holy rollers about what's really going on today in the minds of men. Before I get started, I would like to say that I'm a Christian, and I believe in a Black-African revolutionary Jesus Christ, and I do not believe Jesus will return in my lifetime. I attend church very rarely. I read and educate myself to become more connected with my spirituality. I was brought up to believe in the Baptist/ Christian way of life. When people read this book they'll shout, "How can you call yourself a Christian when you write material like this?" I respond by saying, "There's only one person I'll have to answer to, and it damn sure ain't you."

Now let me explain what I don't believe in and what a lot of men don't believe in, either. I don't believe in the "pie in the sky" theory that you should wait for death to have a good and meaningful life or to be liberated. I believe you can have heaven here on Earth. The only way this can happen is you must first understand the problem.

If you do not have accurate knowledge of the problem, you cannot arrive at accurate solutions.

—Shakari (Author)

The main problem is that African-American women who call themselves Christians have so little knowledge of Christianity, its origins, myths, legends, and history that it is an insult to the religion as a whole for them to even refer to themselves as Christians. To further compound this dilemma, most also refuse to become involved with non-Christian men or men who are progressive, conscious thinkers about religion and Christianity. It's easy to tell a nation of weak-minded people whatever you want to tell them when you know the people themselves have no idea what the truth is.

When the buttons are pushed to make the non-educated blind believer focus on the inconsistencies, flaws, and misinterpreted information in the Bible, the blind believer gets close-minded and defensive and wants to shut out any and all enlightening information. This is in part because the blind believer has been conditioned to live by a lie rather than hear and accept the truth like a child placing his or her hands over their ears and yelling when you try to tell them there is no such thing as Santa Claus.

By believing in the idea of a returning messiah, there is a tendency for people to become passive and accepting of their condition. In this situation, they tend to feel that there is no need to work for change, because God will intervene to make the necessary changes. We then resign ourselves to accept whatever occurs on earth in place of a more heavenly existence; becoming passive and complacent, seeing ourselves as martyrs who will eventually get their just rewards when God finally returns. We should realize that if we keep waiting on this messiah to return, it certainly won't matter, because we won't be here to realize a benefit from this "Second Coming." Although it is believed our souls will be saved and will rise again in some distant paradise. We use this idea of a returning messiah who will liberate us as an excuse to do nothing about our own situation.

—Willis, author

You ever notice it's the friends, relatives, or coworkers with the *least* amount of self-control who become the Bible-toting holy rollers? The same ones who used to smoke weed every day, curse like sailors, have countless sexual partners from both genders, rob, steal, cheat, and would probably kill you dead if you ate their last slice of lasagna, are the same ones who try to preach to someone else on how they should live their life after they so-called "get saved." When you lack self-control and can't manage your own life, you conspicuously place God in charge as to not take responsibility for the future course of your life and decisions. This is called escapism. Women—or should I say most Christian African-Americans, in general—are using religion as a means of escape to mentally rid themselves of the hardships of life because they feel their current situation of oppression is inescapable by all other means.

I think putting a perfect deity that you can't see, hear, or touch first in your life has a slightly sinister connotation. I mean, think about it. How would you react if one day, through the course of general conversation. your child, mother, or husband suddenly admitted to you that they have been so-called saved and that they have someone they consult on all issues before they make any decisions. They love this being above all else, including you, their family, their job, their children, and even their own life. They put this being before anyone, anything, and everything. They talk to it but it never talks back. The being is everywhere. It's omnipotent, but no one can see, hear, smell, or touch it.

Anyone who does not worship this being and live by the rules and guides of its teachings is evil, and your family members don't want to have anything to do with people who don't believe in him, even if it's just friendship. You ask, "Who is this person?" They tell you Shan. Then they show you the book of Shan, which contains all of Shan's teachings on how they should live. I guarantee you'd think they were fucking crazy. Now read this over and replace the name Shan with Jesus.

In terms of how some men look at religion when it comes to women and relationships, a man doesn't want to be force-fed your Bible-toting rhetoric. In the sea of love, the Bible is an anchor plunging you to the bottom of the ocean where there's nothing but despair and loneliness. Don't use the Bible to steer your relationship. Don't be so narrow-minded and assume that the Bible is absolute for everyone because it isn't. Use your mind and your emotions. How you feel about one another is what counts. When I was younger, my mind wasn't strong enough to know the difference between God's word and man's word. As I grew older I became increasingly frustrated with the tripe I was being force-fed by televangelists, preachers, and pastors. I started to do a lot of research and reading on my own. During this time I came to understand that Jesus wasn't born on December 25, nor did he die and return on the dates that most clergymen say he did. There's an eighteen-year silence of Jesus' life in the Bible from ages twelve to thirty. What happened within those years?

There is no absolute description of Jesus, and there are many varying accounts on where he was born and resided. All of these things I speak of are man's best guesses. So, in reality, some of these things and events could be completely wrong. With that being said, I started to think further. Okay, if these things could be wrong, what about the Bible? Are there things in it that could be wrong? Are there things that have been misinterpreted over time—like the fact that maybe Jesus wasn't a virgin and was married to Mary Magdalene? This issue causes much debate within Christian religion sects, among those who are privy to the evidence, because sexuality is defiled in Christianity. If Jesus was married, did he have more than one wife? Did he have any children? Have there been things that have been taken out or rewritten in the Bible to benefit another race or culture? Like the fact that Jesus was a Black man and not European or Caucasian. Even the name Christ has Black connotations.

The earliest gods and messiahs on all the continents were Black. Research has yielded an impressive amount of material on the subject. The Messiahs, some of whom lived many centuries before Christ, had lives which so closely paralleled that of Christ that it seems most likely that the story of the latter was adapted from them. Moreover, the word Christ *comes from the Indian, Krishna or Chrisna, which means The Black One.*

— J.A. Rogers, author

The Bible was also reworded for the Caucasian preachers that Africans are not human and should be used as beasts of burden. Yes, the Bible was reworded during slavery to justify the enslavement of the African. What about the many various gospels that have been completely omitted from today's Bible such as the Gospel of Enoch, the Gospel of Jubilee, and the Gospel of Thomas? These are just a few but there are many more. Are you aware that these texts were read and followed by Christians for hundreds of years before today's Bible? Are you aware that these texts still exist in other Bibles in different parts of the world and also in the Holy Quran? Have you asked yourself why this information has been omitted? Are you aware of the fact that Ethiopia is the oldest Christian country in the world and that Ethiopians were practicing a form of Christianity thousands of years before Christ? Are you concerned at all how this was possible? How can there be Christianity without the arrival of Christ? Are you aware of the fact that the most widely used version of the Bible is the King James Version, which was revised during the time of King James? Are you aware that King James himself was a rampant homosexual? How can someone dare edit the word of God? Are you aware that the old testament of the Bible is basically the Jewish Torah? If you weren't aware of any of these things, then why not? Why haven't you done more research on something that has such a large effect on the way you live your life? Don't you want to know the truth? No, you don't. Most people don't want to know the truth because they can't handle it. As stated before, they'd rather live their life believing in a lie.

Women are putting a perfect deity that no human being—man or woman—could ever match up to first in their lives. Have you even contemplated hypothetically if Jesus did return? You probably haven't. The reason for that is most people don't believe Jesus will return for real; they're just looking for a way out.

The majority of Black people will never be satisfied with a single messiah. No single messiah can be that dynamic. It is similar to a woman expecting a single man to fulfill all of her idiosyncratic wishes, needs and fantasies—it is impossible.

—JAY THOMAS WILLIS, AUTHOR

A weak-minded individual can't stand to be confronted with these types of questions. They have to believe completely and blindly that the Bible and everything in it is entirely true or it breaks down their entire foundation for living their life. In other words, they're lost. They can't function in society without this blind guidance. Think how many times you've opened the Bible and read it. I'm not talking about in church as you read along with the congregation. I mean on your own, on your free time and accord. While reading the Bible, did you ever think, *Hey, this doesn't sound right.* What about, *I think I would have handled that situation differently*? Or *I don't believe that at all?* If you don't, then why not? Why haven't you questioned anything in the Bible? What is your reasoning for the lack of investigation? I'll tell you. Because you've been force-fed by your parents and grandparents since you were young that if you question the Bible, you go to hell. The fear is so deeply imbedded in you that even the most outlandish things in the Bible the average Christian believes without question.

Of course coming to these conclusions didn't happen for me overnight. It took me a very long time to even fathom the thought of questioning the Bible and the God that I've worshiped my entire life. In Christianity this is forbidden. To question God is considered blasphemous. Certain events throughout the course of my life caused me to take a second look at myself and my religion. I was very interested to know why certain things in my life happened or didn't happen at all. When I would ask my so-called Christian friends about it, all I would get was ridiculous euphemisms like, "Sometimes God removes someone from your life to make room for someone else," "God will make a way," or "In everything put God first." What does this mean? Stop dodging the issue and answer the question.

Finally after thirty years, I have the answer. The answer is no one knows. People just say these things to make you feel better or when they don't have any input. Everyone has their own interpretation of what's in the after-life or beyond, but no one really knows. Practically every man with rebellion or ambition is having or is going to have these thoughts, mostly in part because of the passiveness of the Christian religion. A man is aggressive, action oriented, and forceful. He doesn't wait. He just does. The Christian religion teaches one to let things pass, forgive for unnecessary evil, and wait for your reward after death. What about this life? What about now? Your man is thinking the same thing.

Sometimes he wants to knock his boss's teeth out for going over the line or smack some office skank for talking shit or body slam the fry guy behind the counter who fucked up his order because he wasn't paying attention, but most of the time he can't. He has to hold that shit in. If he doesn't release this tension somewhere, your face will be the punching bag. Now do you see the importance of sports, video games, and hanging out with his boys? These are ways he releases tension.

Another thing I found interesting concerning Christian women, or Christians in general, is their total lack of respect for other faiths. How can you have a complete and utter disregard for another faith, which in some cases is much older than your own? They even ridicule and mock other religions as if to say, "How can they believe in such nonsense?" If you back up and take your head out of your ass and the Bible for a second, you can see how other religions around the world view Christians. They believe if anyone is to be ridiculed or mocked, it's Christians because no other religion on the planet claims to worship the actual Son of God.

If you read the Bible regularly, have you read the Quran? Have you studied the Muslim, Buddhist, Mormon, Hindu, or Rastafarian religion? What about Scientology? What about the Five Percent Nation of Gods and Earths? The Five Percent Nation is not a religion, but the teachings are profound and deserve mentioning. Are you scared you might learn something? Have you been informed that there're books that predate the Bible that almost read like a rough draft of today's Bible? Same great flood, similar events and miracles. Do I even have to mention the Epic of Gilgamesh and other scripts that predate the Bible? I really shouldn't because that could spawn an entirely different book, and that's not what this one is about.

I say these things to make this point. From the least educated blind believer to the most highly educated theologian you all have one thing in common: You don't know shit. You're being guided by your faith, and in the same instance being blinded by it. You can't tell me without a shadow of a doubt when Jesus was born. You can't tell me without a shadow of a doubt when Jesus will return. You can't even tell me if Jesus was black, brown, or beige. I don't have to know anything about the Bible or Jesus, and I know that. What's your back-up plan for this foundation of uncertainty? You have none. I don't think you should live your life blindly believing in something that you don't have full knowledge of. But in a nutshell, that's what religion is—faith. Basically you're just following blindly, hoping, praying, and believing, but you don't know for sure. No one does. I'm not saying you shouldn't try to live your life by the teachings of Jesus, but at the bare minimum, open your mind to other possibilities. As a woman, don't close your mind to men who don't believe the same things you do.

An example of this is one day I was talking to some random female, and we got on the topic of religion. I don't really like to discuss religion or politics with just anybody because if your mind isn't strong enough, you can't handle different opinions without getting upset, but hey, she started it. Anyway, she stated that she couldn't marry someone who didn't believe in Jesus. I was awestruck by the absolute stupidity of this statement so of course, I had to inquire further.

"If you met someone who was Muslim, Jewish, Buddhist, or whatever, you couldn't be married to him?" I asked. She stated, "No, because no one can work it out like Jesus." There was no knowledge, basic foundation, or anything backing her statement. She just recited some bullshit that she'd heard from the damn choir. I immediately ended the conversation because I could see it was a waste of my time and brain cells to even try to have an intellectual conversation with this woman.

To me it's like saying if you don't root for my favorite football team, then we can't be together. You both enjoy football, but because he's not a fan of *your* team it's impossible for you to be in a relationship with this person. Ridiculous. As I stated before, I've done a little reading so I know in the Christian belief, everything happens for a reason. How do you know as a woman that a Muslim, Jewish, or Buddhist man couldn't be placed in your life for you to bring him to the light of Jesus? People convert to other religions all the time. It doesn't happen overnight but it does happen. Even some troops in Iraq have converted to the Muslim religion to marry Iraqi brides. You shouldn't go around trying to convert every non-Christian man you meet. All I'm saying is how do you know that God didn't put this man in your path for a reason? You don't know, that's why. You don't know a fucking thing. God doesn't talk to you. You're not an angel or prophet. You can't speak in tongues or predict the future with ninety-nine percent accuracy. You haven't been called to do a damn thing. You think God's calling for you is to work for the government, be a nurse, or to do hair and nails? Hell no. Sit your dumb ass down somewhere and focus. Focus and think.

Like I said, God doesn't talk to you, but you know who does: your pimp of a pastor. There's an old saying that goes, "A preacher or pastor is the closest thing to a pimp." And you follow every little piece of bullshit advice that he preaches on Sunday, don't you? You fall for that shit—hook, line, and sinker. Without a second thought to your own heart and feelings, you follow what he has to say faithfully and blindly. You believe everything your pastor says, and you don't even know the history behind it. You probably didn't even know about the things mentioned in this chapter.

I can't blame you if you're a child. The westernized Christian philosophy is probably all you know and all you've been taught, but as an adult, you're completely at fault. As an adult you have the opportunity to research and question on your own. How can you possibly know everything if you only have knowledge of one piece of the story? It's like trying to learn math by starting with calculus in kindergarten. You'd be completely lost because you don't have the basic fundamentals of arithmetic. It's the same with religion. People are being taught Christianity from the tail end and most don't know anything about the beginning. Nor do they want to. When a man dares to bring up the topic of religion and question certain things, which cognitive thinkers do, women immediately get offended and think he's some sort of devil or demon trying to steer you down the wrong path. In reality he's just trying to make you open your eyes to the wrong road you're already traveling.

You even pass that bullshit on to your family, friends, and kids like a virus without even questioning the validity of the pastor's statements. It's like poison because that's what his words are if you believe what he says without thinking, like poison to your mind. And you know what, oops, you just missed out on your man or future husband. Why? So you can keep giving your pastor that ten percent tithe every month? And while you're cold and lonely at home talking to yourself, mumbling off Bible verses, praying to God that He will send you a man, your pastor is out in his nice Mercedes 500SL that you helped pay for with your tithe money, fucking everything in a skirt. Let me not leave out the ones who are screwing homosexuals. Bitch, you better stop being stupid and start believing in your own heart and using your own mind. Try using your own heart and mind in combination with your religion. When you start to use your own heart and mind, you gain something that eighty-five percent of the entire Black population lacks, which is knowledge of self.

The eighty-five percent who are the "humble masses" are mentally deaf, dumb, and blind to the truth about themselves and the world they live in. Ten percent, who understand much of the truth, use it to their advantage to keep the eighty-five percent under their control through religion, politics, entertainment, economics, and other methods. Five percent, who are the enlightened divine beings, having repossessed knowledge of the truth regarding the foundations of life and of oneself, seek to liberate the eighty-five percent through education.

When you have knowledge of self, you start to see things clearer. Your mind is not clouded by false accusations that make you question your culture and sexual orientation. You begin to see who you are and who everyone else is and how they compare in relation to you, your culture, your race, and your religion. You start to see why African-American men and women can't seem to get along because they have a history that has been stolen from them.

If individuals do not know their past, they have no understanding of the present, nor are they able to conceive of their future.

—Jay Thomas Willis

African Americans now have the opportunity to piece it together, but they refuse to work with one another to bring it to fruition. How can you truly be with someone if you don't even know who you are? Open your mind to other possibilities, like the fact that maybe, just maybe, your pastor might be in it just for the money. He could be a liar or crook. When you follow blindly, you're basically saying to yourself because he says he's a man of God, he's not capable of doing such things. Wrong. If you think that, then you're dumber than I thought and you need to seek further help, far more than just this book.

When you and your man are having problems, do you try to address the argument by using the Bible? He probably knows what the Bible says. He wants to know what you have to say and what's in your heart and mind. I think it says somewhere in the Bible, "Every knee shall bow and every tongue shall confess." What does that mean to you? You know what it means to men? It means me, you, and every good Samaritan, teacher, student, police officer, firefighter, government worker, lawyer, judge, businessman, politician, administrative assistant, CEO, executive, nun, murderer, crook, rapist, thief, thug, pimp, pastor, pedophile, and prostitute will get to have our moment before God and then God, and only God, will decide our fate.

Now do you think if you've led an average life of fairly good intentions but married a Muslim or non-Christian man that you will burn in eternal fire forever when it's possible that a murderer or pedophile can get through the gates? Like I said before, use your own heart and mind. Be a good person in general, not because the threat of eternal fire is looming over your head. Just be the best person you can be regardless, and I'm sure everything will work itself out. Is he a good man? How does he treat you? Do you think he will make a good husband and father? Is it possible that you can come to some common ground in regard to religion? If you can, then what's the problem? These are the questions you should be asking yourself and not just dismissing him because he believes in another faith. If anything, you should be happy that he believes in anything at all. Follow your heart, use your mind, choose your path, and let God guide your steps, not your pastor.

THE BLACK CHURCH IS A HUGE JOKE

The Black church is no longer about religion. Let me rephrase that: The church is no longer about religion. The church is now big business. The reason why I use the term *Black church* is because it's what I'm most familiar with and have the most knowledge of. The Black church doesn't worship God. It worships the almighty dollar. The pastor of the church usually drives a more expensive car than the entire congregation. Try asking him for a dollar to help pay your rent because you're about to get evicted. He'll laugh at your ass and say, "I'll pray for you."

The church is supposed to help the downtrodden, homeless, and needy; clothe those who need to be clothed; and provide shelter for those in need. Try taking your ass to a Black church at night. That muthafucka is locked up tighter than a drum with alarm systems and the whole nine yards. They'll put your homeless ass right in jail if you try to enter a Black church at night.

In my neighborhood alone, they're sixty-eight churches, seven liquor stores, and zero gun stores. Sixty-eight churches in a 9.1-mile radius? Are you fucking serious? Anyone who knows the Maryland area knows this area I'm referring to is not that big. It's only 1.4 miles, according to (city-data.com.) Now notice I didn't say the surrounding areas. I said sixty-eight churches just in one area alone. No wonder Black women can't think straight: They're being bombarded, hoodwinked, and brainwashed by thieves, evildoers, and manipulators—or should I say pastors, bishops, and deacons.

The Black church is a huge joke. It's a minstrel show. They even have homosexuals preaching and leading congregations. What's next? Is the church going to start letting pedophiles teach youth Bible study? How can you have someone whom God himself destroyed teaching you about the Bible? Talk about the blind leading the blind. That's like a pimp trying to preach to a congregation of hoes on how to be nuns. I can just imagine that shit now, the pimp up on the pulpit with his lavender suit, big hat, gators, and cane. Talking about, "Bitches! Bitches, listen! Can I preach to you for a second? You see, bitches, you must close your legs because the pussy…the pussy is the enemy. But hear me, hoes, and hear me well. You still better find a way to get my money!" Think about that shit the next time your stupid ass is throwing money in the collection plate. Please believe that when you're at church, your man is sitting at home watching the football game thinking these same things.

I didn't write this book to debate every verse in the Bible. I wrote it to teach you what some men think when it comes to religion and to help you understand why you should put your religion in perspective and not let it be your sole knowledge base, especially when it comes to getting a man. Some men I've encountered have been brainwashed more than females. They spout off about how we're in our last days and the Bible has predicted all of the current tragedies and unusual weather occurrences. Don't they know that people have been saying that same stupid shit for centuries? God or Jesus hasn't come back yet. What makes you think He's going to do it in your lifetime?

People running off at the mouth with these world cataclysm stories reminds me of the Heaven's Gate cult. The members believed that the time would come when they would be called to heaven, a place that was literal and not just spiritual. Heaven's Gate members believed that a spacecraft attached to the tail of the Halle-Bopp Comet would take them to the Kingdom of God if they lived a disciplined life. They all committed suicide when the comet flew past Earth. Now years later, people are still living their lives and going about their daily business. When people are sitting at home watching the news and they reflect on the Heaven's Gate tragedy they probably say to themselves, *Damn, they were stupid.* David Koresh and the Branch Davidians, Jim Jones and the People's temple, I can go on. All of these nut-job cults say, "This is it. He's coming! The Father is coming back for us! He's coming back to destroy the wicked and give us eternal life in heaven!" Oh yeah? Where are they now?

Not just a few men think this way or have these thoughts. Many do. I know because I've spoken to them. They can come clean and express their beliefs or concerns about religion or other issues when in the midst of other men or a gathering of cognitive thinkers. They will not discuss these issues with their wives or girlfriends. Maybe it's because to date I haven't met, heard about, or spoken to any female with such idealistic thoughts pertaining to religion. This is because of the brainwashing that women have received over the years. It will cause unwanted drama within a marriage or relationship to debate these issues because most of the time women refuse to listen. They close themselves off to the information and will foolishly end the marriage or relationship over these simple issues. It's crazy how women will obey their pastor or boss before they will their husband or boyfriend. Before you think about to whom you should listen, think about who you want to be with forever. Who do you want for the father of your children? Who do you want as your protector and provider? Who makes you feel safe and secure? Who satisfies you sexually? Then your decision should be easy on whose words carry more weight.

I want to make it clear also that I'm not trying to get you to change your religion or anything like that because I don't really care what religion you practice. I just want to give you truth. This is something that most of you have never had. Your only option was to believe the lies you were told. After you receive the truth, if you choose to fall back to sleep, then that's your business, but you can never say no one ever tried to tell you.

9

HOW TO KEEP A MAN (TIPS AND TRICKS)

You've finally settled down and got that man you've always wanted. You're married, or soon to be married, and you're talking about having a family, house, or whatever. Now that you have your man, don't lose sight of what you did to get him. Keep doing all the little things discussed in this book to keep him happy and interested.

One dark secret about men that you need to know is that as a single man who gets into a long-term committed relationship or marriage, it's shocking to his system to now have to focus on sex with one woman for the rest of his life. It might sound simple for women, but for a single, sexually active man who is used to going out and getting random pussy on any given night of the week, it's hard to go cold turkey with just one bitch. There's no known cure or remedy for this. No matter how sexy a woman is, how wet her pussy gets, or how good she can give a blow job, a man will eventually get tired of having sex with just her. It's sad but true. This has absolutely nothing to do with women. It's men and just how they're made. When I was younger and I got involved with this female who everybody else around my neighborhood was trying to get at, an older friend said to me, "Yeah, you got her, but you will get tired of fucking her."

I said to him, "Man, you must be crazy. I'll never get tired of hitting that. She's pretty, she's sexy, and she's fun to be with."

"Okay, we'll see," he said.

I found out much later that he was right. The sex was good, and she was sexy and everything but it was just the same. A good way to prolong this inevitability is variety in sexual routine. Just as you think about what you should make him for dinner, also think about what you should wear to bed. Think about what you should wear when he comes home. You don't have to do a bunch of elaborate shit. You can be sexy and comfortable too. Some tight booty shorts and a wife beater will do just fine, and it doesn't even have to match. The trick is just to put on something that will entice him, attract him, tempt him. If you feel comfortable enough to wear it around his boys when they come over, then it's probably not that alluring. Hint: Try to never wear anything cotton to bed unless you're on your period or it's *extremely* sexy. The way silk, satin, or other exotic materials fit the contours of a woman's body is very tantalizing to men. Cotton doesn't do this unless it's skintight.

Try giving your man a call and leaving a sexy voicemail or text message on his phone describing what you want to do to him when you see him or how good it was the night before. Don't forget that you left the sexy message either, because he will play that shit over and over at work so by the time he gets home your ass better be wet and ready. Don't start slacking and wearing dumb shit to bed like cotton pajamas with fruit on them, big yellow Tweety Bird slippers, and an old Aunt Jemima head wrap, talking about I want to be comfortable. If you start saying to yourself, *I don't feel like dressing sexy tonight*, it's like your man saying, *I don't feel like getting my dick hard for you tonight or ever.*

You should be trying to keep your man turned on at all times. It's not hard. Think of a man's sex drive like a returning appetite. Just as he must eat to satisfy his normal craving for food, he must also satisfy his sexual appetite. It is a natural human response. When a woman dresses sexy, it's like an appetizer to her man's sexual appetite. Don't fall into the trap of thinking, *Well, he isn't doing the same for me* or *It's fifty-fifty, and he should be trying to turn me on at all times, too.* Wrong. In this situation it's a double standard, and that's something you will just have to deal with. You just need to concentrate on your part right now.

This book is intended for women to learn. The average man knows most of the issues discussed within. Get your shit in order as a woman. The average man will start to reciprocate automatically. If he isn't, then take a long look at yourself first before you look elsewhere. If you feel that you're doing everything in your power to keep a man, keep the spice in the relationship, and attract him, and he still isn't responding, then there may be other underlying issues with him that need to be addressed. That's when you can start pointing the finger, but not until you have your shit in order. If he's not even meeting you halfway in trying to keep the spice in the relationship, then you need to get his ass a book that you think will help the situation. You never know, I might write another one detailing the issues that females have.

COOKING

This is where a lot of common sense factors into keeping a relationship together. When a man and a woman are in a relationship, they are supposed to do for each other. If you can't depend on the woman you're in a relationship with, then who can you depend on?

Why do a large percentage of women believe when they do certain things for a man they're submitting? What ever happened to just doing your part? In a traditional relationship or marriage, the man is the protector and provider, and the woman is the nurturer and keeper of the house. I don't see how submission became a part of the equation. You're supposed to be in a partnership. One partner has responsibilities and so does the other. Neither partner's responsibilities is more important than the other. If you don't do your part, then there is no need for you to be there. If you don't cook, don't clean, and don't bring in any money, then you're basically just a fuck buddy. How are you an asset to the relationship? Do you think you're an asset just because you have a pussy? As a woman, what do you think your part is supposed to be? Do you believe it's the same as the man's? If so, then this is probably a major contributing factor of why you're still single.

Women who believe their position in a relationship is the same as the man's are perfect examples of what I mean when I say women have lost touch with their feminine side. What happened to just being the best woman you can be?

When it comes time to cook for your man, don't ask him, "Do you want something to eat?" The question should be, "What do you want to eat?" Of course he wants something to eat. Don't ask him. Have that shit ready. Didn't your fat ass have something to eat? What makes you think he's not hungry? He has to eat every day just like that rest of the world, right? Well, get your ass in the kitchen and cook. After you've fixed something for him, if he won't be arriving for a period of time, don't leave it with the rest of the food. Have his portion set aside in a plate or container covered and labeled. Leave a note letting him know you've fixed something for him.

He doesn't care about your day or what gossip you heard at work on an empty stomach. If you don't cook every day, then you need to cook when it counts the most. Simple things mean a lot to men. Fixing him a sandwich after he comes in from playing sports or while he's watching TV is always good. Making him a light snack after sex is a way you can score huge points with your man. Usually during sex a man is going to expend two to three times the amount of energy than a woman—especially after ejaculation.

Some men will even cook dinner, lunch, and other meals. Personally, I love to cook, and I enjoy the taste of my own cooking. There are men who can cook and don't mind doing it. Just because your man enjoys cooking doesn't mean you should take that shit for granted. Even if your man likes to cook, you should be preparing and serving the meals at least three days and nights a week. Don't take his kindness for weakness.

TODAY WAS A GOOD DAY

If you ever wondered what a good day for a man would be, just keep reading, and this will give you a clear idea. A good day for a man would be to wake up around noon to his woman giving him oral sex, which would then lead to regular sex. The morning sex session would end just in time to catch the last few minutes of the pre-game show. His favorite sports team would be playing their archrivals. While he showers and shaves, she prepares brunch. His woman serves his plate, and he eats while watching the game. His team is triumphant after a hard-fought battle. He calls up his friends who are fans of the opposing team to boast of his team's victory. His woman comes into the room shortly after and starts to give him a victory blow job. They have some victory sex, and he falls asleep in the bedroom. A few hours later he awakens to the smell of his favorite dinner being cooked. He heads to the dining room where she prepares his plate. During dinner they have a *brief* intellectual conversation on a subject they both enjoy. He then goes into the living room to catch the late game, read, or watch the program of his choice. After that, he heads to the bedroom where his lady is relaxing in something sexy. She has recently showered and is smelling seductively succulent. He closes the door and cuts off the lights because now it's time for a four-hour sexcapade. Today was a good day.

DO YOU HAVE YOUR MAN'S BACK?

Men are more action-oriented while women base their emotions and love on material and superficial things like money, jewelry, and clothing. A man understands that to show his love for a woman he must buy her something. This is what's accepted in the female mind as the man having love for her. She doesn't know or doesn't care how to show her love for her man. I personally think it's the latter of the two. A man is going to judge your love for him by what you do, not by what you buy him or say to him.

Here are some examples of expressions of love that a man will appreciate and won't forget:

- Totally supporting him when he loses his job without ever complaining, nagging, or giving him unwanted advice; making him something to eat while he watches the game *without* being asked and not fixing yourself anything in the process. This may sound trivial but the gesture is letting him know that you did this for him and not because you were thinking something like, *I'm going to make myself something to eat. I guess I better make him something too.*

• Showing your loyalty to him while in the presence of others. A hypothetical example of this is if one day you both invite friends over for dinner. After dinner everyone decides to play a board game. Your man is up, and he answers the question incorrectly. He denies the answer is incorrect and would like to verify it within the rules of the game. You know for yourself that his answer is definitely incorrect but you take his side anyway. While the other players are preoccupied looking through the rules, you quietly whisper the correct answer in his ear. This is showing loyalty and solidarity as a couple. In other words, you're my man and in every situation I have your back.

10

NOT ALL WOMEN ARE CUTE, SEXY, OR BEAUTIFUL

Who let these hoes in my room? A lot of women I've spoken with seem to have an overblown sense of their own beauty. Society has preyed on the emotions of women and somehow made them believe that they're all beautiful in some way. This is a complete farce. That's why there's such a thing as supermodels and women who shop at Lane Bryant and Ashley Stewart; Lamborghinis and Hyundais; condos and mansions. They are completely separate, and they're separate for a reason. One is overwhelmingly better than the other; there's no comparison. So to say *all* women are beautiful, I think, is an insult to the women who truly are. It's also an insult to the intelligence and general vision of men.

Do you consider yourself a ten or dimepiece? If so, are you a model, actress, or in some occupation that typifies beauty? If not, why? Do you think men view you as a ten or dime? If you think you're beautiful, then take your ass to any popular musician's video shoot and audition. I'm sure most women would reconsider their personal thoughts on their own beauty after they've seen the competition at those shoots. I think the percentage of beauty on Earth is completely exaggerated and women are the ones who are making these outlandish claims. You may be hot, phat, or sexy, but we're talking about beauty here.

Let me give you an example. While a cameraman was scanning a crowd at a football game, Pamela Anderson was discovered. In a stadium of thirty thousand or so, she was the only one in the crowd considered to be beautiful enough to catch the eye of some executive who then in turn had her pose for an ad. And the rest is history. I'm not claiming that Pamela Anderson is beautiful by any stretch of the imagination. I'm just using her discovery as an example. Let's get that shit straight from the jump.

Okay, let's do the math here. I hope I'm doing this right—I was never really good at math—but let's say using the Pam Anderson example that there's one beautiful person in every thirty thousand. What would be the percentage of beautiful people on Earth, whose population is over six billion? If there was one beautiful person for every thirty thousand that would mean about 3.5 percent of Earth's population is beautiful.

When a man thinks of a woman's beauty, he completely separates the fine women from the average ones, and the average from the ugly. Each is not even in the same neighborhood. An okay chick isn't going to rise to the level of a fine chick or dime-piece just because she gets her hair and nails done. It must be some other shit going on that makes her just okay.

Weight is a very important issue with men, which you've already gathered by now, I hope. Only men with fetishes pursue large women. They're called Chubby Chasers. Of course big women will still get play, but that's only because in a man's mind the larger you are the easier it will be to fuck you. Men are well aware of a women's ability to have children and that she's going to put on weight over time after having kids. The question on his mind is how much weight. If you're a borderline large woman right now, imagine how much weight you're going to retain after twelve years and three kids. Please believe that men are more than just a little worried about this. Between males we try to gauge what a woman will look like over time by looking at her mother. If her mother is fat and busted, then that's what his ass is going to be stuck with after fifteen years of marriage. That's why it's important as a woman to stay in shape.

When I checked the BlackPlanet, Blackpeoplemeet, Match, BET, Happily Single, BlackPersonals, and Black Voices sites for research purposes, I clicked on a lot of names like SexyinDC or CutiepieSingle and HotRedbone, and they all have one thing in common: not one of them is cute, sexy, or hot. Not all women are cute, sexy, hot, or even attractive for that matter. Society has implanted this into the brains of the masses to help build their self-esteem.

Please believe when I tell you there're some boogerbears, sausage eaters, mudducks, and silverback gorillas out there, and it's not just a few. There should be a certain criteria obtained among third-party perspective before a female can just call herself cute, sexy, or attractive because apparently a lot of women who think they are attractive aren't. Somebody has either told them wrong or they've disregarded all the laws of human sexuality and basic physics and started using these names for themselves erroneously.

If a female is overweight then that's three strikes against her. That's right, I said three. I will explain more later. There are some pretty women out there who're overweight but they're pretty in the face only. So if you have this issue, then you need to specify with names like CutefaceinDC, Neckup10, or Cutefacehugewaist—something like that. But you can't call yourself attractive because you don't have the whole package. Men don't look at a female with a cute face who's 239 pounds and say, "Oh, she's attractive." You say, "She's cute in the face, but that's a huge bitch."

See, when men mentally evaluate a woman, depending on the man, he'll start with the body or face. Usually it's the body. The face is usually judged all in one but the body is judged in three to six parts, depending on what he can see. The three main parts on which men judge the female body are the breasts, stomach or waist, and butt. The three lesser parts are the arms, legs, and feet. If you're overweight, then right there you have three strikes against you because who can judge a body when it all looks like one big blob. If you have a phat ass, nice breasts, and a huge gut, then that's how you're seen by men. When two men are talking to each other, they will have a conversation sort of like this:

"Yeah, dog, the broad with the phat ass called you today."

"Yeah, she does have a phat ass, don't she?"

"Yeah, she does but she got that huge gut, though."

"I know. That's why I haven't called her back yet. I'll hit her up later on when I don't have shit else to do."

Your flaws will be pronounced, especially when it comes to turning him on. If you're turned on and your man is not and he doesn't have any medical issues preventing him from getting an erection, then that's your fault—not his. It's your responsibility as a woman to turn a man on. If you think just by looking at your naked body that men are supposed to get aroused, then you're definitely confused about your female role. That shit may have worked when he was a young virgin and inexperienced but not with a man who has had ten to twenty women. If you want the dick, then act like you want it. Don't just lay there thinking, *Something must be wrong with him if he can't get hard.* Ah, no, sweetheart, there's something wrong with your big stank ass.

Because while you're lying there doing nothing, that man is probably thinking, *My dick won't even get hard for this broad. I'll just make her play with my dick for a little while until it gets hard so I can fuck and get the hell out of here.*

There's a reason why he can't get hard, and the reason is you. When he pulls back the covers and sees all those rolls, when he snuggles up close and he smells that stank breath, when he plays with the pussy and it has a grotesque odor, that's why his dick isn't getting hard. If you stimulate the penis correctly it will become erect. It's that simple. Just as when a clitoris is stimulated correctly a woman will get wet. So when a man is unable to become erect, and it's not a medical issue, that means it's a mental one. He's either not turned on by you or something is causing him to be disgusted or turned off.

11

WHAT IS A REAL MAN?

Ah yes, the real man, the ever-present phrase that females generally use to describe an indescribable entity. What is a "real man"? How do you define him? How do you define any man for that matter? Some say real men pay their child support. Bishop T.D. Jakes and the U.S. government agree that real men should pay their child support. I don't listen to either one, by the way, but notice they didn't say anything about spending time with the child. So what is a real man? Women use the term *real man* all the time. How would a woman know what a real man is? She wouldn't.

A woman would have no clue what a real man is. The reason is because there is no such thing as a real man. There are only men. Regular, average, above average, below average, middle of the road, basic men—that's all there are. The term *real man* is an illusion. It's a metaphysical being generally used by women as an insult to men because they know there's no earthly way men could ever live up to the term. The term *real man* is used so loosely to describe all sorts of things from men who don't cheat to men who love fat women. Have you heard this before? "If he was a real man he would get to know me and not judge me on looks alone." "A real man takes care of his kids." "A real man would love me for me and he wouldn't try to change me." "Any man can be a father but it takes a real man to raise a child." "Real men don't hit women." All these are bullshit phrases that I've heard to the point of nausea. So many times I've heard this same shit over and over. Is a real man one who pays two thousand dollars a month in child support but doesn't have a hand in raising his child or children? I say no. The government says yes. Some women say yes also. Is a real man one who has a hand in raising his children and pays child support but demeans, abuses, and molests them? I think not. So back to my original question, what is a real man? There isn't a clean definition for this term. Every person has their own definition of what a real man is or should be. If there ever was such a thing as a real man, then in this day and age, he's dying, and women are killing him. The way they are killing him is the way that the male child is being raised. The way women raise their male children is making him less and less masculine. This is a major factor in the increase in homosexuality and men on the DL. The male child is being raised effeminately. This stems from history and conditioning over time.

Most women don't want a so-called real man, a masculine man—a man who takes charge, doesn't take lip from his woman or anyone else, and does what he wants to do without her consent or anyone else's. These men are not called real men. These days the term *bad boy* is used by women to describe these men. A lot of women want someone who's in touch with his feminine side, someone who shows compassion to others and little cute furry animals, and can discuss his feelings with them daily, someone who cries at movies and wears socks and sandals with shorts. Sound familiar? It should because these are effeminate traits. What man has these traits and is not homosexual or has the potential to be?

Let me explain a little of how I came up as a young man, and maybe you can see the difference between today's men and me. When I was young, we used to play a lot of sports in our neighborhood. Mostly it was football and basketball. Of course in the inner city there's always going to be a tough time finding a piece of well-kept land within walking distance that will accommodate ten to twenty young men who want to play football. If you're lucky enough to find one, there will always be someone who complains. It never fails. A church field, school yard, large median strip, or some random home's backyard, I've been thrown off all of them. So as a young man, what do you do? You want to play football with the fellas but you don't have anywhere to play.

I'll tell you what we did. We played tackle football in the street. That's right. We used to tackle one another on hot pavement and concrete. No padding, nothing on to protect us from the street. Some people had on shorts and some didn't. It depended on what you were wearing at the time. We called this Murder Ball. Bloody elbows and knees; stitches in the face, hand, and leg; running into parked cars while looking in the air for a pass; nose bleeds; running into high-tension telephone wire—I've seen it all happen. And you know what would go on when something like that happened? No one cried. Everyone gathered around to see if the player was all right and not hurt too bad. He usually took a break on the sideline to recoup from whatever injury had occurred, then he brought his ass back in the game to play.

Don't get me wrong. Occasionally when something like this would occur it would be game over and the dude would end up going home or to the hospital. But this didn't occur often. Usually he would come back in the game. There were always one or two dudes who never wanted to play, and you know where they'd be? They'd be down the street playing Double Dutch with the girls. So already you had a pretty good idea of who was going to be a fagela when they grew up. Are real men starting to emerge here? Nowadays if someone's child comes home and needs stitches and his mother asks, "What happened to you?" and the child responds, "Tyrone tackled me in the street," before he can finish explaining she'll probably be on the phone to the police. The next thing you know it would be on the seven o'clock news with a headline like, "Teens playing violent sporting games in the street. Is your child one of them?" This is the type of world we are living in today. This is the same type of shit that is turning young boys into bitch-made ass-men in combination with the Willie Lynch syndrome—another subject for another time.

One day while playing football I fell on a brick and cut my knee. I didn't have my bike so I had to walk home with blood running down my leg. The gash was so big and deep you could see the bone move in my knee as I walked. I was young and didn't know what to do about it at the time. My cousin was home, and I displayed my injury and asked, "What should I do?" You know what my cousin told me to do? "Go lay down." Then as I lay there bleeding, my cousin brought me a towel to put under my knee to soak up the blood. That would probably be unheard of today.

Of course about an hour later my mother arrived and was frantic at the sight of my leg. She took me directly to the hospital where my knee required eight stitches to close the wound. That's one of the reasons why my favorite number is eight. I thought it was really cool at the time to have eight stitches. I showed them off to everyone I could. People would "ewe" and "aw." I acted like it was nothing. When I went back to the hospital to have the stitches removed the nurse asked me if I wanted a local for the pain. I told her no. Deep down I wanted to see what it felt like to have the stitches taken out. I was mentally testing my own manhood as a young child. It wasn't painful at all except the initial tug where the flesh had intertwined with the string. The doctor had to cut and pull several times to remove all the stitches. It was a weird feeling. I've never felt anything like it since. Is a real man being formed here?

We used to do all kinds of adolescent shit. But these are the things that boys do. As young men we'd do things like go out in the woods and try to shoot rabbits, squirrels, and turtles with BB guns. We used to feed Alka-Seltzer to birds and watch them explode. Today if you did this, a child psychologist would tell you that this behavior is the beginning of a person who will grow up to be a serial killer. Society no longer lets a boy be a boy or a man be a man. I'm not saying that growing up this way makes you a man but at the very least it makes you tougher than today's so-called metrosexual. It used to be if you had a beef with a dude in school at lunchtime or after school, you would go settle that shit in the bathroom, the middle of the lunch cafeteria, schoolyard, or wherever. Sometimes it was during lunch and after school, and with the same dude or two different ones. When the teachers heard the commotion, they'd come running, and of course, you'd get disciplined for fighting, but it wasn't such a big deal. You'd get detention mostly, and if it was your third or fourth time, you'd get suspended. But that wasn't the worst of it. The real discipline came when the principal called your parents at work.

Suspension and detention, I can handle, but please don't call my mother. As a child that's what you'd be thinking. Growing up, I'd seen enemies in school who used to hate each other and fight all the time. After they would get in trouble a few times at school and their parents found out, they would end up squashing the beef and sometimes become best friends. It wasn't because they suddenly had an epiphany and came to like each other. It was because they were both tired of getting disciplined at home by their parents. I've seen fathers and mothers come up to the school and give their child a spanking in front of the class. You wouldn't have a problem out of that child for the rest of his years in school. Do parents who care and are positively involved in the lives of their children create real men? Today the police would be at the school and Child Protective Services would take the child away from the parent for an incident such as this. In the years that I was in school, if you were ugly, then you got ridiculed. If you were a fat girl, you went to the prom alone or you didn't go at all. You graduated from the sixth and twelfth grades, not every grade. That's just how it was. Now they tell you that everyone is beautiful when they aren't. They tell you that everyone's a winner when they aren't. They tell you that everyone is special when they aren't. I think a lot of women, or people in general, have an inflated sense of self-worth.

The point I'm trying to make is that people used to be human beings and handle their own problems. Back when I was growing up, if you were fat, you didn't blame Burger King. If your dumb ass spilled hot coffee on your lap while driving, you didn't blame McDonald's for making the coffee too hot. If you were violent, you didn't blame *Tom and Jerry* cartoons, movies, or video games. Nowadays people want to blame someone or something else for their problems. This is what women do when they can't get a man. When Black women can't get a man, they call themselves strong, independent Black women. I think this is an incorrect term because there is no such thing as an independent woman. It's more like angry, alone, and frustrated. Angry because of the mistakes they've made with men. Alone because no man wants to deal with them or the attitude they exhibit. Frustrated—sexually frustrated—because they can't get the kind of attention they want from men.

So as a man living in today's society, the best way for me to describe a real man is one who takes a hundred percent responsibility for his own actions. As a child, if you were teased, you would be hurt by the teasing but most would develop some sort of defense, whether it be teasing back, which was the most popular, beating up the person or people that teased you, or coming back to school a new man because over the summer you gained weight and shot up a few inches. This happened now and again. The ninety-eight-pound weakling, who everyone picked on because they could, would come back to school three inches taller and fifty pounds heavier. He wouldn't even have to say anything. His new physique gave off the flashing neon sign of don't fuck with me. That was survival of the fittest, weeding out the weak from the strong. The point is you figured out a way to survive, and you moved on. You didn't retreat to your room with the rest of your carnival-freak friends and form a plot to murder the individuals who shunned you. You got through it, and you found a way to continue. Is this a real man? One who deals with his problems head-on? One who triumphs over adversity? Men are being emasculated more and more every day. I read somewhere that the genetic material that is needed for a man to become a man has been shrinking with each passing year while the genetic material that is needed for a woman to become a woman is growing. When I found this out, it was shocking but I wasn't surprised. At this rate everyone will have a pussy in a thousand years.

A lot of women set the bar impossibly high when it comes to

dating, comparing men to a fictitious Jesus-like figure that they've created in their minds. Believe me, this changes drastically with age as the realization of a life alone starts to set in. In a female's youth when the ass is phat, the stomach is tight, and the breasts are perky and she's getting hit on everywhere she goes, she usually has no perception of the future. A woman in her twenties might want a man with a nice car, a house, and a master's degree, but by the time she reaches thirty, she'll be satisfied if he just has a car that works. By the time she reaches forty, she'll be happy just to find a man who is healthy and can walk to her house from the bus stop. By age fifty, she'll be satisfied with any man who isn't dead.

12

SEX

Do you want to keep your man interested in sex? Then give him oral sex—face down, ass up, deep throat that shit, hold those legs open, and don't be scared of the cum. What are you doing to keep your man interested in sex? Men get turned off just as women do. Those old-ass pajamas with the holes in them and those beat-up panties and bras that don't match—why are you wearing that shit? Do you think it's attractive? If you can't afford anything else, then believe me it's far more of a turn-on for you just to be butt naked than to start getting lazy and wearing some whack shit.

Men separate sex and love and never the two shall meet. There's only physical pleasure for men when it comes to sex. There is no emotional connection. That's why it's perfectly fine for you to be as nasty as you want in the bedroom with your man because he isn't going to look at you any differently when you're outside of the bedroom. As a matter of fact, it should be considered mandatory to be extremely raunchy with your man. That's what a man wants anyway—a whore in the bedroom and a lady in public. Throw all of your inhibitions out the window when you enter the bedroom. All the kinky, nasty, filthy shit you only think about doing you need to let happen in the bedroom. For you stuck-up,

Christianized, brainwashed holy rollers, even the Bible tells you that this is okay. When you initially have sex with a man, don't reveal every one of your perverted sexual desires all at one time. Slowly expose your freaky needs layer by layer over time in your den of iniquity. This will keep him interested in you sexually much longer, and it also won't scare off someone who is not as experienced as you are.

ORAL SEX

Fellatio, head, a blow job, suck my dick—are you a novice or an expert? How do you know? Do you even care? Women really need to learn and practice more on how to give a good head job because I think it's becoming a lost art. A lot of women think they can just put their mouth on a dick, and it's supposed to feel good. This is incorrect. There's a lot more that goes along with it. When you give a man oral sex, don't just go through the motions. You should enjoy giving your partner head. Let him hear how much you enjoy it between various slurping sounds. Tongue kiss the tip of the dick exactly like you would kiss his lips. Act like you've been in the desert for three days without food or water and the dick is a Popsicle. You wouldn't just run up to the Popsicle, bite it and chew it down. You would lick and suck on it and savor every last drop. Treat the dick the same way. Do you know one major reason why you should enjoy giving your man oral sex? Because the more a man is turned on, the bigger his dick gets. That's right. Now I'm not saying if your man has a four-inch dick it will swell to eight inches. You can just forget about that shit. I'm saying if a man is highly turned on, then his erections will be fuller, stiffer, longer, and harder.

I know you've probably heard about or been told to practice

on a banana, cucumber, Popsicle, or something like that. Those are all good but another much better technique would be to practice on your own fingers—your index and middle fingers. This way you can feel if your teeth are scratching or scraping your fingers. Multiply your teeth scratching your fingers or an accidental bite times a hundred because that's how the pain is going to feel to a man's dick. Imagine someone biting your clitoris or scratching it with a dry fingernail, and you can imagine what a man must feel when you accidentally scratch his dick with your teeth or bite it. Practicing with your fingers will also give you a very small idea of the type of pleasure a man is feeling. Just like the palm of your hand is more sensitive than the back, the same goes for a man's dick. The underside of it is much more sensitive than the topside. Just like your fingertips are more sensitive than the base of your fingers, the same goes for a man's dick. The head is more sensitive than the base. Roll your tongue around your fingers, simulating as if they were a dick. Flick your tongue across the tips of your fingers simulating as if it was the tip or head of a dick. Think about your clitoris and how you like it licked. Lick the head of a dick the same way.

The hand motion you use is important also. The way you jerk or pump the dick is important because most men can't cum without you physically pumping the dick. You can make him hard with just sucking it, but it's very unlikely he will cum if you're not jerking him off at the same time. Here's a good way to tell if you can give a good head job. If you can make a man cum in a reasonable amount of time without him having to do anything like jerk his own dick or move your head up and down when you're giving him oral sex, then you can give good head. If it takes him forever to cum while you're giving him head or he has to intervene in some way to get himself off, then you have a lot of work to do. This doesn't mean you give bad head. You just need to fine-tune the shit.

Don't forget about the balls, a usually neglected area. This is a very sensitive area, so be careful. If you're just starting out at giving oral sex, you should probably steer clear of this area until you've mastered the penis. Providing pleasure to the balls is a more advanced technique. If this area is handled incorrectly, it can cause a lot more pain than pleasure. Sucking gently on the balls or fondling them gently provides great pleasure, but remember, this is in combination with everything else. This is the reason God gave women two hands and one mouth. You use your mouth and tongue to lick and suck the dick, use one hand to pump it up and down and the other hand to *gently* play with the balls.

WHY A MAN WON'T PERFORM ORAL SEX

There could be any number of reasons why a man won't perform oral sex on a woman, but the *number one* reason is because of poor hygiene. If pussy smelled like roses and tasted like strawberries, you couldn't stop a muthafucka from eating you out. He would be down there all day and night, but unfortunately it doesn't smell or taste like that. All pussy has a smell to it no matter how clean it is. It's a very distinctive smell. The smell isn't necessarily bad, but as a man you just have to get used to it. Pussy is an acquired taste and smell, just as coffee and beer are acquired tastes where you have to drink it more and more until your palate adjusts to it. That's why for a woman, having good hygiene is key. Also there is no delicate way to tell your mate that she's rank if you ever find yourself in that situation. Imagine having to tell a woman that you like that her pussy stinks. Most men just leave and give a lame excuse why it didn't work out. I had this female friend I used to hit every now and then. During sex when she would perspire she would have this odor to her. It wasn't a horrible odor but it wasn't that good, either. Imagine me telling this chick, "Hey, ah ya know what, when we're having sex...um...you stink." Yeah right. If we ever had sex, after I told her, she'd be horrified. That would be the only thing she would be thinking about. I never told her. I just stopped seeing her.

Taste is an essential part of oral sex. How a woman tastes is important because if your man is giving you oral sex, and he says it tastes bad, it might be a sign of infection or something else. To help you in this category, you may want to eat more fruit, exercise regularly, and not smoke, drink obsessively, or do drugs. Sweating is a way the body cleanses itself of toxins, so exercise regularly. Also be aware of any medications you might be taking. They may contain ingredients that your body may secrete. A doctor may tell you eating more fruit or what you consume doesn't have anything to do with how you taste. But remember doctors also used to think that drilling a hole in your frontal lobe would let sickness escape from your body and cure most diseases. I don't see how a doctor could say that what you consume doesn't have anything to do with how you taste or smell because I think the consumption of alcohol would be a definite contradiction to this. Anyone who knows someone who drinks heavily knows when that person comes around they smell like liquor regardless if they haven't been drinking. I'm sure oral sex with a female who drinks and smokes a lot would taste different than one who didn't.

I'm not a doctor but all I know is I used to be involved with this female who ate a lot of fruit, usually five servings a day, like an orange and apple at breakfast, some pineapple at lunch, and a peach and mango at dinner. She was religious about the shit. Fruit was like her chocolate. Whenever I would kiss her lips, lick her skin and nipples, or give her oral sex, she would always taste sweet. I haven't tasted a woman like that since. As I said before, I'm not a doctor but common sense told me that the fruit had something to do with the way she tasted, and even if it didn't, five servings of fruit a day is recommended for overall good health.

THE SOUNDS OF PASSION

Making noise or moaning in the bedroom is always a plus. Use the filthiest language you know when in the bedroom, but don't talk too much. Running your yap during sex is definitely a turn-off. Just express how you like it, what you like, and how you feel. Who wants to be having sex and hear nothing from their partner? The lights are out and you're obviously in the right mood, so express yourself verbally. Don't just lay there like a limp noodle. Noise is the way men gauge if you're enjoying yourself. If you make noise when he hits a certain spot, then he'll return to that spot.

It's also how you make noise that's important. Most women will moan and groan and do the "whoa, baby" thing and maybe call out a man's name, but when a woman makes noises, squeals, moans, and screeches that are signature to her, that's what turns a man on the most. That's what will make him come back for more. A woman who sounds like a lemur every time she cums is definitely going to have a man come back for more than one who doesn't. Why do you think the retired porn actress Janet Jacme was so popular? It was because she seemed so into the sex and she expressed herself verbally—it was a beautiful thing. If you have no idea who she is, then buy one of her videos and see for yourself. You never know; you may learn something.

Initiate sex often with your man. If possible, always try to be first at bat. This will turn him on tremendously. A man always has to be first to initiate everything in life. Often he gets tired and wants to relinquish control to someone else. This is where you come in. You should be flattered and feel appreciated and proud that your man has surrendered control to you. It's not often that a man willingly gives up command of anything. For a man to give up control to you is showing you that he likes and trusts you. This is not something he's going to do for everyone. Resigning power over himself is only reserved for the people he fervently trusts.

Think of it as if you were sixteen and you've just gotten your license and your father lets you drive his prized car that he's polished and driven sparingly since you were a child. Think of how thrilled and grateful you'd feel when he placed the keys in your hands and you sat behind the wheel. Think of how proud you would feel that your father had that much trust in you. This is how you should feel when your man trusts you enough to let you be in charge of things. He may never express these particular words to you, but that's how he's feeling. Don't be afraid to ask for sex or even beg for it. The more you want it, the more he will want you.

Even if you aren't actively sexually involved with anyone, you should at least take time to study sex. What I mean by that is you should know what to do when the time comes, and you should be comfortable doing it. Read or watch films on females you know men like. Why do you think men like a particular female more than another? Most of the time it's the sex appeal. A female could be gorgeous but men may like seeing another female more than her because of the other woman's sex appeal.

LAZINESS

You better get sweaty and pop that pussy. Don't just lie there and receive pleasure. Your man expends a lot of energy trying to please you, so you should do the same. Being lazy is a turn-off, especially when the female is on top. If you like it slow, that's cool. Just make sure when you get on top when you start to do your thing, take it slow and make it deep and rhythmic. This is the time when it's more important for you to make yourself happy. Being on top is really the only position where the female is in command. So take advantage of your time while you're up there. You should be trying to make your ass touch your back—bend that spine and pop it. Command that position so well that he likes you being on top so much that it turns into his favorite position.

Know where words are appropriate. In the bedroom, certain phrases turn men off. I know this comes as a shock as probably most of this book has, but yes, certain words and phrases will turn a man off while having sex. For example: *Let's make love. Make love to me.* These phrases will turn men off even if he does love you. The number one reason is because it sounds like some White commercial television shit. That phrase is not nasty enough for the bedroom. It should be more like *fuck me*, *let's fuck*, or *come get this pussy.* These are more appropriate phrases for the bedroom. Yeah, that last one is a good one. I'm turned on right now thinking about that broad Tawny Dahl (Pandora) in the movie *Baby Boy* who said that shit. Anyway, ah… moving on.

Other phrases not to use: *What are you doing? That's not it.*

What the hell are you doing? Direct him to the right area if you need to. You don't have to announce it to the world. If that's not the right spot, then tell him what is. Let him know. Don't sit there like he's supposed to be an expert on *your* body. Everyone is different. What turns one person on might not turn on another. If what he's doing isn't working, then you need to show him what does work. Keeping it to yourself isn't going to help anything.

WOMEN SHOULDN'T HAVE ANY UNFULFILLED SEXUAL FANTASIES

Why in the world would a woman have any unfulfilled sexual fantasies? It makes no sense to me. It makes me think that maybe women aren't comfortable in their sexuality. Whatever sexual fantasies you have, your man will fulfill. There's no need to hold them in. If you want your man to fuck you hanging upside down while wearing your old prom dress with one sock on, believe me he'll do it. Whatever you want to do sexually, your man will do. Don't hold it back. If you have to hold your sexual desires back, then maybe you need to reevaluate the relationship.

WHY MEN CHEAT

Why do men cheat? It's a formidable question. There can be any number of reasons why a man would cheat. The main reason is because we like sex and we like it with different women. Just think of it as you going to your favorite restaurant. The food is always good, the service is excellent, and the price is very reasonable. No matter how good the food and service is, if you had to go to that same restaurant every day, the odds are you'll soon tire of it. It has nothing to do with the restaurant. You just want to try something new—new scenery, new types of food, new servers, and a new environment. It's the same for men. In many cases it has nothing to do with a particular woman a man is with at the time; it's just after a while a man is going to get tired of having sex over and over with the same chick.

Another reason why men cheat is problems at home. If you're nagging him all the time or causing unnecessary drama, he is going to seek out a more drama-free woman. Men have to deal with enough conflict at work and in the street. They don't want to have to come home, and battle with their women, too. When your man is not being satisfied sexually, what do you think he will do? If he wants his dick sucked and you won't comply, do you think he's going to wait for you to change your mind? Hell no. Every time he's working late, he's getting his dick sucked. Every time he tells you, "I'm hanging out with the fellas tonight," he's getting his dick sucked. Every time he tells you, "I'm about to go to the store. I'll be back," and he comes back five hours later, he's getting his dick sucked. What you won't do, another broad gladly will. Men are action-oriented individuals. They don't wait for things to come to them; they go out and get what they need. What is the reason that you're not giving him oral sex? You need to explore that question. If you're not satisfying your man sexually, then you should expect him to cheat.

13

I DON'T NEED A MAN

"I don't need a man"—the lonely woman's mantra. How many angry, sexually frustrated, manless women say this to themselves daily? Wow, now how many times have you heard these phrases? I know for me the figure has to be in the hundreds. *I don't need a man to complete me* or *I don't need a man to define who I am*. Both are sorrowful statements from dejected women. Are you one of these women who uses these phrases? Some people call this a syndrome similar to the ASS or Angry Sista Syndrome described by Jamal Sharif. I've heard females regurgitate these same comments on talk shows, on the phone, in articles, on the Internet, in discussion groups, and while having personal face-to-face conversations. Every female that I've seen, heard, or read about who uttered these words had one thing in common. Every last one of them was single. I've never heard a female who was married or in a committed relationship say "I don't need a man" or "I don't need my husband." I believe it's "angry single female" code speak for "I'm frustrated that I'm alone." They're alone and they don't know why. I believe single females feel this phrase is empowering. They think it's the men who're at fault, but what's contained in this book will let them know different. They need some way to justify the fact that they're single. So they proclaim, "The reason why I'm single is because I don't need a man." Well, if women continue to think this way, then they really won't need a men because they'll never get one—at least not one of any substance.

Webster's Dictionary defines the word *need* as *A condition or situation in which something is required or wanted*, i.e. *crops in need of water; a need for affection.* In essence when women respond, "I don't need a man," they're saying to all men, you're not required or even wanted. Why would a female say, think, or believe such stupid shit when she's single and looking for a man? Basically she's saying I don't need a man, but please marry me. I don't need a man, but I want a baby. I don't need a man, but give me child support for our illegitimate offspring.

What the fuck is wrong with you? Are you stupid or just ignorant? Who wants to hear that they're not needed, wanted, or required? Stop listening to dyke logic. Women seem to fall for this way of thinking because they think it will liberate them somehow when in actuality it constrains them. Once you fall for this way of thinking, in order to justify it, you have to live by it. Now you have to subtract men from your everyday life and pretend that a man is not required in your life until you meet one. I'm here to tell every female out there that you do need a man. It clearly states this in Maslow's hierarchy of needs—a psychological theory depicted as a five-level pyramid of what a human needs to become self-actualized or reach complete happiness. He also talks about the pyramid levels in terms of homeostasis, the principle by which your furnace thermostat operates: When it gets too cold, it switches the heat on; when it gets too hot, it switches the heat off. In the same way, your body, when it lacks a certain substance, develops a hunger for it. When it gets enough of it, then the hunger stops. Maslow simply extends the homeostatic principle to needs, such as safety, belonging, and esteem. He sees all these needs as essentially survival needs. Love and esteem are needed for the maintenance of health. He says we all have these needs built in to us genetically, like instincts. In fact, he calls them instinctoid.

Love/Belonging needs

After physiological and safety needs are fulfilled, the third layer of human needs is social. This involves emotionally based relationships in general, such as friendship, sexual-relationship, or having a family. Humans want to be accepted, and to belong to groups, whether it be clubs, work groups, religious groups, family, gangs, etc. They need to feel loved (sexually and non-sexually) by others, and to be accepted by them. People also have a constant desire to feel needed. In the absence of these elements, people become increasingly susceptible to loneliness, social anxieties, and depression.

If you're lacking one of the needs in the hierarchal pyramid, then you are deficient. Of course as a human being you can still function: A swimmer can function without air but eventually must come to the surface to breathe; the body can function without food or water but eventually must eat and drink. Yes, it's possible to function without a man or meaningful relationship. But eventually you must obtain this need in one way or another or transfer the desire to some other task in life—becoming obsessively involved in church or volunteerism or becoming a workaholic, alcoholic, drug addict, or developing an eating disorder. These are ways that the need for a man are suppressed and controlled but never completely subdued. The need still remains.

As I continued to read the definitions for the word *need*, I found another definition that I thought was quite interesting. It means "to be necessary." This was interesting because a person can argue that mostly everything on earth is necessary. To completely block out and believe that a man is not needed, required, wanted, or necessary in one's life, I think, puts women in a very pathetic state of mind. What is life without someone to share it with? Why are a lot of women so afraid to admit the truth to themselves? Women need men just as men need women. A lot of women will get very technical with the word *need.* They make the argument that women say "I don't need a man" because when you say you need something it's like saying it's something you can't be without or something required for survival. When they say that, I tell them, "You don't need clothes, soap, toothpaste, and money to survive, but you have them." It's the same thing with a man.

The only things that are actually required for human survival are food, water, and shelter. I believe that a rewarding relationship with the opposite sex is a necessary asset to a healthy and happy survival—physically and mentally. Right now a lot of women can't see the future past the next workday, but I'm here to tell you that you better open your eyes and look deeper. Think about when you're eighty-five and you're with your significant other. You're both sitting on the couch in the living room during a family get-together. Your children and your grandchildren are all around you. Everyone is so pretty and handsome. They're smiling and looking so happy, making noise and having fun and just enjoying your company and life in general. You both look around at the legacy you've created, and the good, educated, proud, attractive, naturally righteous people you've molded. You both turn and look at each other, at your elderly, embattled, wise faces. Thinking back almost sixty-five years ago when you first met, you embrace each other joyfully. Tears stream down your faces.

The youngest of the grandchildren toddles over to you and gently taps you on the knee and asks, "What's wrong, Grandma?"

You respond, smiling, "Nothing, baby. Grandma is just happy, that's all." You pick him up and place him on the couch with you. You look at his young, innocent face, knowing that he'll become a man one day, and you hope he'll be as good a man as the one sitting on the couch with you. That's what your lives will be about. That's how you'll be remembered—not your career, business, how much money you made, or how independent you claim to be, but the type of people you were. Your legacy will provide a foundation for centuries to come as your family flourishes and multiplies. A relationship with a significant other will be the most rewarding and important thing in your life. Men need women, and they're not afraid to say it or admit it. The majority of a single heterosexual male's actions in life are geared toward the pursuit of women. Get rid of your negative thinking. You will never—and I repeat *never*—get a man if every day you tell yourself you don't need one.

14

MAN SPEAK

I'm going to give you a little education on urban slang or Ebonics when it comes to men. I don't like to use the terms *slang* or *Ebonics* when it comes to describing African-American inner-city language because it's basically just African-Americans substituting for the language that has been lost. But I will use them here because these are the terms that everyone has become accustomed to hearing. Besides, Ebonics is a language because your language is what you speak when at home. It comes from the Western part of Africa. Ebonics is an African intrusion on the English language, when we spoke certain African languages that didn't contain vowels, only consonants. But that's another subject for another time. I break down Ebonics or slang in several categories:

Commercial Ebonics—The terms you hear on radio and television that the average person can figure out.

State Ebonics—For each state that has an African-American population, the urban dialect will be different. If you're not from that state or you don't visit there often, you probably won't know the dialect.

Neighborhood Ebonics—For each neighborhood within a state where there is an African-American population, the urban dialect will be different than the next neighborhood. For instance, in D.C., I'm mainly familiar with the Southeast area. Just by talking to someone for a short period of time, I can pretty much tell what part of the city they're from.

Above are the three main urban dialect categories, but it goes further. There is also a dialect associated with gender. There are slang terms that males use exclusively, and there are slang terms that females use exclusively. I'm going to educate you on some terms that men use to describe women. I can only give you a few because what may mean one thing to me may have another definition in another city or neighborhood. Besides, I can't reveal all of our secrets.

As you know, men watch a lot of sports. In sports you usually have players who start the game and others who come in later. There is usually one exceptional player on the team, which is the star. The starters are usually the next best players on the team. Below is how a lot of men describe various women defined in order of importance.

THE ROSTER, also known as my roster, my team, or the lineup: these are his various women. A typical lineup for a man would be a star, an ace, two starters, and a roster bonus or MILF—mom I'd like to fuck.

THE STAR, also known as the superstar, winner, wifey, main, he may also substitute his favorite celebrity's name for yours. For instance if he thinks Nia Long is attractive, which is definitely not a debate since we all know she is, he may refer to his favorite female as Nia or Miss Long. The star is the female the man is grooming to become his wife or serious girlfriend. She is usually the one with the coolest personality but not necessarily the best body or the prettiest. She's the one who's there when he needs her, and she puts him at the top of her priority list. He defers to her first at all times unless she's on her monthly cycle or in-her-feelings at the time. This is where you want to be.

THE ACE, short for ace in the hole or ace-boon-coon, also known as my ace, my dog, my roll-dog, my nigga, my bitch, ghetto queen, thug miss, the rock or pit—short for Rottweiler or pit bull—and just recently my Lil' Kim because of how she kept her mouth shut and took the rap. This is the female who is usually down for whatever. She smokes with him, drinks with him, parties with him, will have sex almost anywhere. She'll knock another female out if he tells her to—and won't ask any questions about who it was—and if the feds run up into the spot, she won't say a word. There is usually always an ace on a man's roster. Deep down inside, a man is usually a bit fearful of the ace because she is the one he can be himself around, which leaves him the most vulnerable. The ace can skyrocket to the star position fairly quickly but she is also the hardest to tame. He is also concerned who else's ace she may be since there is usually no commitment. She also isn't readily available; she may come up missing for a few days at a time.

THE STARTER, also known as the bun, bun-bun, or my girl, these are the females who can move into the star position if the star herself fucks up. When a man is talking to his friends he might refer to you as such but you probably have no idea what he is talking about. Usually the starters get utilized most in the winter. In the summer a man may clear his entire roster to make room for fresh starters but the star remains on the team. This a common practice among men. When the spring and summer arrive, a healthy, sexually active, heterosexual man doesn't want to be tied down to just one woman.

THE SUGAR MOMMA, grandma, sweets, also known as a MILF (mom I'd like to fuck) is pretty much self-explanatory. This is an older female who hits him off with a little cash or gifts every now and then, and he breaks her off some dick. She knows the situation and doesn't step out of bounds. A lot of times the sugar momma is married but her husband either is never home, ignores her, or isn't laying the pipe the same as he used to. All she's looking for is some good sex from a younger man, no strings attached.

ROSTER BONUS, also known as bonus or plus, is the female who knows about the star and maybe a couple of starters but still wants to be a part of his team. A lot of times she may be bisexual, and she's looking to hook up with the star or one of the starters and him. A roster bonus is hard to come by, but is always a welcome addition.

BENCHWARMER, also known as backburner, on simmer, or on ice, is a female who may have been a star or a starter previously but for any number of reasons has lost her spot. She also may be a female who is on the bench because a man may have too many players and needs to rid himself of one before he can bring her off the bench. A man may refer to another man's entire lineup as benchwarmers as a form of ridicule. There can be any number of reasons why you're riding the pine. You can tell your status by his actions. Where does he spend the majority of his time? Does he cancel other plans to be with you? If he has a traditional schedule, where are his Friday and Saturday nights spent? These nights are usually reserved for the star.

INJURED RESERVE is a female who has sunk past the benchwarmer spot and could be on her way off the team completely. She still has a chance to stay on the team but the current terms of her situation with the team owner have to be renegotiated.

WAIVED, also known as cut, is a female who is no longer with the team.

These terms are used by men in the company of other men to describe females. Sometimes they are used to disguise a conversation on the phone or in public. What category are you in?

15

WHERE ARE ALL THE GOOD MEN?

I hear a lot of women asking this same question: "Where are all the good men?"

Where do you think? They're everywhere. They're all around you. Everywhere you go, they're there. Have you picked up your head and looked? Are you a good woman? Do you have *your* shit together? Your chances of meeting a good man are not very good if you're a two-hundred-pound waitress who works at Chuck E. Cheese. Are you in shape? Are you making yourself available to be approached? Are you giving off signals as if you want to be approached or are you holding your head down, not making eye contact, and talking obsessively on the cell phone everywhere you go? You can meet a good man anywhere. The question is do you want to and are you trying to meet one. Are you expecting every good man to come up to you? Why should they? Why should good men approach you and single you out? Why aren't you approaching them? How many good men have tried to talk to you but you just dismissed them without a second thought?

EXAMPLES:

Ron is putting himself through college to get his master's and has two jobs, one at Blockbuster and the other at Pizza Hut. He may have been that good man for you, but you dismissed him when he approached and tried to talk to you because you didn't respect his current occupations. Now Ron has graduated and is making a six-figure salary as VP of sales at a well-known mortgage firm.

Darnell quit his job and moved back home with his mother, sold his car, and maxed out all his credit cards to start his own business. He may have been that good man for you, but you dismissed him because he didn't have any money or transportation to take you out. Two years later Darnell's business is flourishing, and he plans to expand.

Raeqwon has a middle-class job and one child. He may have been that good man you were looking for, but you dismissed him because you don't date men with children. Raeqwon coincidentally ran into one of your girlfriends the week after he met you, and she didn't dismiss him. Now a year later they're married and just moved into their new home.

Good men are everywhere. You should be evaluating your standards. Are they reasonable or do you have an outrageous view of your own self-worth? By the way, all these examples are taken from true-life experiences from my friends and colleagues. I've changed their names to protect their identities.

As a woman you have to open your mind to more than the stereotypical datable man. Look past a man's occupation and get to know the individual before you make the decision that you can't date him. Look past a man's material possessions and find out who that man is inside before you dismiss him for not having an expensive car, overpriced clothes, or a fancy home. Men accept the shortcomings of women all the time. As long as a female is attractive to him, a man doesn't really care where a woman works, where she lives, or how she dresses.

The victims of Hurricane Katrina are a perfect example. These people have been scattered throughout the country, most don't have a permanent home, clothes, a vehicle, a job, or basically anything. They're starting their lives over from scratch. What would you do if you met a Katrina victim who was your type? Would you dismiss him because of his situation? What's the difference between a Hurricane Katrina survivor, and a man who has had a personal disaster of his own—for example bankruptcy, some trumped-up-lawsuit in a kangaroo court, or outrageous mother support payments?

Put down the remote and stop watching Lifetime and other shows that fuel your hatred toward men. Don't you see that's how they make their money, by living off your stupidity, emotional blindness, and lack of willingness to learn? Go out there and get your man and stop being brainwashed by your single, desperate, childless friends, and family, or else your stupid ass is going to be in the same situation they're in when you get their age.

I can't tell you the exact place you should go to meet good men because there is none. Good men are all around you. You just have to open your eyes and look. Open your mind to more places to meet men other than church and the grocery store. Church is the last place you want to go to meet a good man because the good, conscious brothers aren't going to be there. You may run into a good man in the club, a bar, as a passenger in a car, on the bus, at the neighborhood McDonald's, at your child's summer camp—you may meet him anywhere. Stop falling for the same dumb, cliché bullshit that you've heard over and over for years, like all the good brothas are locked up, homosexual, uneducated or drug addicted. Think about who's feeding you that garbage because African Americans own very few public broadcasting companies.

When I take my son to football and basketball practice, I see nothing but educated, conscious brothas taking an interest in their child's life. I see just a handful of mothers. There can be anywhere from fifty to one hundred fathers at practice or the exhibition games cheering on their child. Open your mind to something else other than what you've been force-fed. I know the club isn't the ideal place most people think of going to meet good men, and by no means am I telling you to start going, but let's use a little common sense here. Think about how many people attend. Do you really believe that every brotha in there is "no good"? If your stinking ass is in there, then you're "no good," too, right? What about your friends or family members who may attend? Are they all "no good"? Just use common sense wherever you happen to meet someone. Get to know them before you make a snap decision about their datability.

MONOGAMY AND COMMITMENT

Monogamy and commitment, the two words in the English language that men hate and fear the most. Can a man be monogamous? Can he be faithful to one woman? If he was a former playa or has had many sexual partners in the past, can he totally and completely commit himself to just one woman? The answer is yes. Yes, he can. This is not a myth. It *is* possible for a man to be committed and monogamous to one woman. A woman must understand that this is not an overnight process. This is a long-term, day-by-day, step-by-step process.

Reflecting on the pussy-as-a-drug analogy in Chapter 2, if a man was a heavy user, you wouldn't throw him back into the party scene and expect him not to relapse just because he's married, right? You'd have to slowly bring him around your single friends and other attractive women. You don't want it to be a shock to his system. This is where a lot of women make life-altering mistakes.

Women seem to think because a man is married he automatically becomes monogamous. Wrong! He is still a man. He has the same natural urges as when he was single. It takes time—a long time—for a man to train himself to commit to one woman. I personally feel it's unnatural for a man to be committed to one woman for life, yet this is the accepted practice by westernized society today. Since the dawn of time, men have had multiple wives and partners. Kings and emperors have had harems and concubines, Biblical characters have had multiple wives, and even U.S. presidents have openly had a wife and mistress. When did it become morally wrong to have more than one wife? Was it the jealousy of women that changed this or religious fanaticism? Either way the practice of polygamy needs to be further explored in these modern times.

YOU CAN'T FORCE A MAN TO COMMIT

A lot of women seem to think they can force a man to commit. They try different things such as sex, food, money, and even getting pregnant to ensnare men. You can't force a grown man to do anything he doesn't want to do. He may lead you on to believe that you can, but this is only a technique used by men to deceive women. The best way to get your man to commit to you is simple: trust him. Don't nag him into a situation where he feels he's already being accused and convicted of something he hasn't done. Then he might as well do it to reap the rewards of what he's been impugned for. Don't forget about having everything else in order.

If you're being open-minded sexually and you're having sex with your man regularly, it will be that much harder for him to cheat. Let me explain a little of how our bodies work. If a man is having sex regularly, then the urge to go out and search for a new sexual partner is very faint. If he's having sex irregularly, then the urge to have sex is average or normal. If he's not having sex at all, then the urge is much like a starving fat man at a buffet. That's why I tell women all the time who ask me questions about men: "If you're not having sex with your man, you should expect him to cheat." Let your man commit to you. Don't try to force or rush him.

MEN FALL IN DEEPER LOVE THAN WOMEN

A woman can fall in love many times within her lifetime. A man, on the other hand, is going to fall in love about three times maximum in his lifetime. Men usually fall in love the first time very early on in life—between the ages of twelve and sixteen. Anyone who's been in that situation can tell you that young love is the most heart-wrenching of all. This is how your pimps, playas, and gigolos are made. Usually if a man falls in love with a girl in his youth and she shuns him, he won't put his heart out there again for a very long time. He'll likely become a pimp, playa, or gigolo and just use women because of the hurt he's feeling from having his heart broken. Disregard all the bullshit you hear in the hip-hop world that "I was born a playa or pimp." That's total bullshit. Unless he came out his mother's pussy with a suit and gators on, then that muthafucka learned how to be a pimp and playa just like everybody else.

During his teens or early twenties a man may fall in love again. If it works out or not determines the next time he puts himself out there. After the third time he puts his heart on the line and it doesn't work, that's a done deal. You won't have to worry about that man trying to fall in love ever again.

MEN TELL THE TRUTH MORE OFTEN THAN YOU THINK

When a man tells you, "I like you, but I don't want a relationship right now," then you better damn well believe him. Don't think six months later he's just going to change his mind. When he tells you, "I have a girlfriend but I still want to see you," and you accept this situation, then you need to act accordingly and know what you are. You are a concubine, pussy to be fucked at his leisure. Don't expect nor should you be surprised that you don't get the same treatment he gives to his girlfriend. The reason why a lot of men are so straight up with women is because a lot of women don't listen. Men know they can come right out and say most things because a woman will only hear what she wants to hear.

16

THE OTHER WOMAN

I have no idea how a woman can sense tension in a relationship, but some broads sniff that shit out like bloodhounds. Not only do women sense tension but they seem to pick up on exactly what's wrong in a relationship. This amazes me. There can be many things wrong in a relationship like communication, sex, or selfishness. Some women have an uncanny ability to sense exactly what's wrong and key in on it, especially when they want the man bad enough. Let me give you a scenario, and maybe you can better understand.

Deshan is seeing Nicole. They've been seeing each other regularly for about nine months. Nicole is reluctant to give Deshan oral sex, and she doesn't cook for him. When she does get around to giving him oral sex, it's quick and mediocre. In the beginning of the relationship, it wasn't a big deal, but now it's become an issue for Deshan.

He goes to work one Monday, sits at his desk, starts working on his computer, and goes about his daily business. Toya walks by his desk and says, "Hello." Deshan knows Toya from work. They speak to each other regularly and have daily non-work-related conversations. You could call them office buddies. Their relationship up to this point has been strictly platonic. Toya senses the tension. "What's wrong with you?" she inquires.

"Nothing."

"It must be something wrong because usually you're all friendly in the morning."

"I'm straight. I'm just not feeling too good."

"Un-huh. I know what it is. It's that new girlfriend of yours, isn't it?" Deshan glances up at Toya but doesn't respond. "Yeah, I already know because I can see it all in your face. What, is she acting up already? Let me guess. She talks too much, right? She's too needy? Oh, I know. She won't go down on you?" He glances up again but still doesn't say anything. Toya responds, "You don't have to say a word. It's all up in here." She gestures with her hand toward Deshan's face. "I bet she can't even make a decent sandwich—that's if she cooks for you at all. I never have a problem doing that for my man, especially if I'm getting treated well. I enjoy pleasing the person I'm with in that way." Toya looks around, gets closer to Deshan, and in a low tone says, "I even bought some movies for us to watch together so I could learn more about how to do it better. And cook, please, after me and my man broke up I had to start taking food over my girlfriend's house because I was so used to cooking for two."

Guess what? Nicole just lost her man. Who's Deshan's new girl? You guessed it—Toya from work. You think it doesn't happen like that? You think women don't come at men like Toya came at Deshan? You think Toya's a man-stealing tramp, and it's not that easy? You might be right about the man-stealing thing, but this is how the game is played. Toya knows that two things can happen: Either Deshan will reciprocate or he won't. This happens to men all the time. It doesn't happen every day, but it does occur more often than you might think. I don't care how ugly your man is, how much of a bum he is, or how fat he is, there's always some chick waiting in the shadows for you to fuck up.

17

THE AFRICAN-AMERICAN MAN'S BURDEN

How do sistas look at African-American men as opposed to all other men? Do they hold their men in high regard as other races or do they betray and ridicule them? The Black male holds the Black female in very high regard, but I don't think the same can be said for the Black female's feelings toward the Black male. The main thing most modern-day African-American women don't seem to understand is the African-American man has been portrayed to be the most despicable, depraved, loathsome human being on the planet, and all other races consider him to be the most revolting. African-American women of all people should know this, but because of their total unquestioned assimilation into westernized culture, most have denounced these indisputable facts as conjecture.

I'll give you an example. One day I was flipping through radio stations, and I came across a popular morning show where a Mexican porn actress was being interviewed. The host asked the actress if her parents knew of her illicit lifestyle. The actress replied, "Yes, they do."

The host asked, "How did they find out?" The adult actress said her brother bought a sex tape, saw her on it, and then told her mother about it. She went on to say that her mother called her frantic about the news she'd gotten from her brother and asked her if she'd had sex with a Black man yet. The actress said,

"No," and her mother, relieved, stated, "Just don't have sex with a Black man, and I can accept what you do." This was the adult actress' reasoning for not having sex with Black men on tape.

Now this pyorrhea-mouth, wetback skank is essentially nothing more than a paid whore and even the allure of financial gain won't convince her to have sex with Black men. What does that say about the African-American male? This is how we're being portrayed around the world through misinformation by the American media and other sources. Even her toothless hag of a mother calling from her dirt-floor hovel in some bacteria-filled part of Mexico has a misguided view of the African-American male.

African-American women of yesteryear knew of this racist way of thinking without a shadow of a doubt because discrimination was up close, in their face, and personal. Now since racism isn't as overt, African-American women seem to think this type of treatment is over or no longer exists. If you believe that there isn't any more racism toward Black men, any hatred or separatism, then you're sadly mistaken and hopelessly lost. Racial discrimination is still very much a part of everyday life for Black men. What do you think happened to the four million registered Ku Klux Klan members and their offspring? I stressed the word *registered* because how many more believed in the same ideals but weren't card-carrying members? How many African-Americans believe in the ideals of the NAACP but are not registered members? Can you fathom that? You think they just walked through a portal to another dimension? The Klan doesn't call itself "The Invisible Empire" for nothing. Has the offspring of the Klan turned into what is now known as the neo-Nazis who once tried to march in Illinois until violence erupted?

Black women seem to miss this entirely because in today's

society they have it easier. There are more programs aimed to help and empower women who have the law on their side, especially when it comes to sexual crimes, and most people are usually willing to give a female a helping hand.

This is not the case for men, especially Black men. Black women think because they're able to purchase a home on the opposite side of town that everything is equal. Black women believe this completely until something happens to them to shake up that safe world, to take them out of that comfort zone, to make them stand up and take notice. Then all of a sudden they want to become the next Fannie Lou Hamer overnight. They think, if I can make it, he *should* be able to make it also. Black men are well aware of the division between the races because they deal with it every day. They think because our voices are deep and bass-filled that when we speak with emotion we're hostile or angry. They think because our "good hair" is kinky, coarse, or curly that it's dirty and unkempt. Think about how many obstacles will be put in a Black man's way as opposed to a Black woman's. Think about the fact that if it's hard for a Black woman, it's going to be ten times harder for a Black man. Think about in the course of your own life and employment history how many Black male bosses you've had, then think about how many were White men, White women, or Black women.

In this westernized society, the Black woman has become docile, passive, and complacent. She has completely conformed. The Black man will *never* completely conform to a westernized lifestyle. It's just not in his nature. The ones who have are called Uncle Toms, coconuts, Oreos, sell-outs, and yams. Almost everything the Black man does is in rebellion toward a westernized way of living—from the way he wears his hat and clothes to the way he walks and talks. Study your history and realize what has been done to you. Only then will you be able to heal and start to correct the problems. How can you start to correct anything if you have no idea what the problem is? Study your history and genealogy. Whatever will help you on the path to finding out who you are, do it. I'd think an individual would carry himself differently if he found out he was a direct descendant of Pharaoh Akhenaten, Queen Nefertiti, or Jesus, no matter what level of society they're currently in.

Instead of trying to force your man to conform, you should be encouraging him to rebel and follow his heart and his own path. Those who rebel are seen as troublemakers, cowards, and separatists in the moment of rebellion, but as the dust settles, they are seen as revolutionaries, innovators, heroes, and leaders. Martin Luther King Jr. rebelled against racism. Muhammad Ali rebelled for freedom of religion. Nat Turner rebelled against the unimaginable horrors of slavery. Uplift, support, and empower your man. Don't drag him down because of your brainwashed beliefs. The opposite also rings true. If he is a soft, milquetoast wannabe then you need to leave him alone and get with someone who isn't a coward and has a backbone. Don't settle for some unconscious metrosexual who kissed just enough White ass to get that six-figure job he isn't qualified for, and will drop your ass in a second if you in any way compromise his professional position. Hold out for that strong conscious Nubian brother you've always wanted. This brother doesn't have to worry about conforming to any westernized philosophy because he uses his own mind and has his own ideas. Why would you want an unconscious slave anyway? What type of woman does that make you to accept a man of such poor quality? Work hard to become your man's helpmeet, not his liability.

18

YOU KNEW HE WAS A BUM WHEN YOU MET HIM

When a woman meets a man and he tells her that he's a drug dealer, he has a girlfriend, or he has four kids by four different women, why is she then all of a sudden surprised when he hurts her or the relationship doesn't work out? You knew he was a bum when you met him. You decided to be with him for whatever reason. So don't all of a sudden get brand new when he hurts you. You knew the deal when you first met him. Don't get me wrong. Anything is possible. A former drug dealer can change his ways, conform to the system, and take the business savvy that he learned from the streets and apply it to corporate America. This has happened in the world of business and hip-hop several times. But think about how often this happens and how many don't make it out the game. How many times have you heard the phrase, "I'm a stripper but I'm only stripping to pay my way through college?" I personally don't know any successful former strippers. Do you know any? You could be one. If so then you're one in a million. Success doesn't mean you have your own car and apartment, either. That's just getting by—I mean graduating from college in your chosen profession, getting a job in that profession, or similar, and you're excelling in that profession. Someone who is not living paycheck to paycheck, has a home, and is preparing to start some sort of business in the next few years—that's being successful to me.

If you're prepared to accept what you know about him in the beginning, after it doesn't work out, don't turn around and blame good men that you meet in the future because you chose to deal with a bum. All men are not dogs. Those men that you chose to deal with were dogs. Don't blame your bad decisions on good men. You chose to deal with Janitor Tyrone who has never had the same job for more than three months, has six kids by six different mothers, but he looks good and eats your pussy every night. You chose to deal with thirty-five-year-old Robert who doesn't have a car, still lives with his mother, and doesn't plan on leaving, but he buys you nice things. Of course he can buy nice stuff for your dumb ass because the momma's boy doesn't have any other expenses. You chose to stay with hot-tempered Byron who has a job and his own place but is a total slob, smokes weed, drinks every day, and argues and demeans you every chance he gets. You chose to be with Pretty Tony who has been in college eight years and still hasn't declared a major. He also gave you a venereal disease and blamed it on a public restroom toilet seat. You believed him, and you stayed with him because he looks good on your arm and all your girlfriends are jealous, but if they only knew.

Tina chose to stay with Ike and Whitney chose to stay with Bobby. It's up to you as an individual. Just don't bring that baggage with you into the next relationship when this one doesn't work out. A good man will be more apprehensive to deal with a woman if he knows she's dealt with a lot of bums. He doesn't want to have to sift through all that baggage to find the real person. He doesn't want to have to prove himself unnecessarily, either. It's a waste of his time, especially for a man who has his shit together and feels he's a real catch. Don't try to hide the fact that you've dealt with a lot of bums either, because it's going to come out in your attitude.

For example, I was dealing with this female for a minute. It wasn't much of anything—she was just a booty call every now and then when I got bored. I could tell she was starting to catch feelings because she would always want to go out or do other things and not just fuck. I usually never went out with her, but one day she wanted to take me out for my birthday, and I agreed. After she'd treated me for my birthday she dropped me off at my house. About half an hour later she called me back, talking about, "Where's my wallet?" I thought she was joking around, and I didn't know what she meant until she said, "Where's my wallet? I know you took it."

"What are you talking about?" I said.

"I always leave my wallet right between my seat and armrest in the car, and we were the only two in the car, and now it's gone."

I paused for a minute because I thought she was playing around, then I became sick to my stomach at her accusation. I told her point blank, "You know what? I don't have your wallet, and I don't know what happened to it. Also, don't call me anymore because I can't believe that you would even think I would steal from you."

She said, "That's fine with me. I won't call you anymore, but I don't think you stole it. I know you did. I've looked everywhere for it, and it's not here. Now where is it?"

After that, I hung up on her. I just sat there awestruck that this rotten-tooth, weave-headed, shit-face baboon would have the audacity to accuse me of stealing her wallet, which probably contained three dollars inside a fake Gucci purse. I couldn't understand why she would do that when I made three times more than her at the time, and if I wanted to, I could buy and sell the wench like a Chinese slave. I didn't get that she thought I took her wallet because that's not something I'd ever do. Then as I thought about why she reacted the way she did, it came to me that she must have dealt with a lot of sorry men in her life. And sure enough about two hours later she called me crying and apologizing. She'd found her wallet, and she begged me to keep seeing her. Of course I didn't even contemplate seeing the tramp again. She admitted that she'd had her wallet stolen before by some dude she used to deal with, and she thought the same thing had happened again. Boo-hoo, blah, blah, later for you, skank. What did that shit have to do with me? Did I ever give off the impression that I was a wallet thief? No, I didn't give off that vibe. It was her and her idiosyncrasies. She brought that baggage with her from a previous relationship. That's what messing with bum-ass men does to women. They think because a few dudes in their life have been worthless that all men are bums. Wrong! Review your track record and look at when you first started seeing that person. What bum features did he have that you accepted?

19

AFRICAN AMERICANS AND STDs

When it comes to relationships between African Americans, I think the situation concerning STDs is vital. In this day and age, you have to protect yourself, and wearing a condom is not enough. There are diseases out here that even condoms won't protect you from. You have to communicate with your partner and take precautions with everyone, no matter how much you like, love, and trust them. No matter how you feel about the other person, he may not even know his own status. Right now I'm going to discuss the most serious disease that commands our attention. The AIDS epidemic is killing everyone, but it's killing Africans and African Americans, in particular. These are statistics concerning African Americans, according to the Centers for Disease Control:

HIV/AIDS AMONG AFRICAN AMERICANS

The HIV/AIDS epidemic is a health crisis for African Americans. In 2005, HIV/AIDS was among the top three causes of death for African-American men aged 25–54 years old and among the top four causes of death for African-American women aged 20–54 years old. It was the number one cause of death for African-American women aged 25–34 years old.

DENIAL

Studies show that a significant number of African-American males identify themselves as "DL" or on the down low. As a result, they may not relate to prevention messages crafted for men who identify themselves as homosexual.

PREVENTION

Among all people in the United States, the annual number of new HIV infections has declined from a peak in the mid-1980s of more than 150,000 and stabilized since the late 1990s at approximately 40,000, according to the CDC.

Minority populations are disproportionately affected by the HIV epidemic. Blacks make up about 13 percent of the U.S. population, according to the 2000 census. However, in 2005, they accounted for 18,121 (or 49 percent) of an estimated 37,331 new HIV/AIDS cases in thirty-three states. In 2005, Blacks accounted for 20,187 (50 percent) of an estimated 40,608 AIDS cases.

In addition, the main transmission category for Black men living with HIV/AIDS in 2005 was sexual contact with other men while the primary transmission category for Black women with HIV/AIDS was high-risk heterosexual contact.

To reduce further the incidence of HIV, CDC announced a new initiative, Advancing HIV Prevention (www.cdc.gov/hiv/partners/AHP.htm), in 2003. This initiative comprises four strategies: making HIV testing a routine part of medical care, implementing new models for diagnosing HIV infections outside medical settings, preventing new infections by working with HIV-infected persons and their partners, and further decreasing prenatal HIV transmission.

The following are some CDC-funded prevention programs

that state and local health departments and community-based organizations provide for African Americans:

• A program in Washington, D.C. provides information to and conducts HIV prevention activities for DL men who don't identify themselves as homosexual. These include a telephone help line; an Internet resource and a program in barbershops that includes distribution of condoms, risk-reduction workshops, and the training of barbers to be peer educators.

• A program in Chicago provides social support to help difficult-to-reach African-American men reduce high-risk behaviors. It also assists high-risk women with culturally appropriate, gender-specific prevention and risk- reduction messages.

It's scary to see that the number one cause of death for African-American females is AIDS. And that they are twenty-three times more likely to contract the disease than White females, according to CDC. That shit is not only sad, it's horrifying. Heroin and crack are killing our babies before they're even born; and AIDS, heart disease, diabetes, and murder are taking them after they're born. An editorial in *The Washington Post* revealed that if D.C. were a country, it would be ranked eleventh in the world for HIV prevalence.

C'mon now. The nation's capital is running neck and neck with the Third World countries of Africa for the highest HIV rate? That shit is ridiculous. As African-Americans, we must understand that this disease is out there, and it can happen to you. And we need to better understand that there are people who have it, know it and are still having unprotected sex.

Here's a story from my past that drives home my point. One day I met this random chick around my way. I got her number, and we started talking. She wasn't all that cute, but she had a flat stomach, nice-size titties, and a nice little ass. I called her one day, and we decided to meet for some drinks. We started talking, and the topic of sex came up. So during this conversation I asked what her HIV status was. She said, "You know what, no one's ever asked me that before." Then she continued, "We're being real here, right, so let me let you know that I've been HIV positive since I was six years old. I contracted the disease from a man who raped me."

Let me tell you, I felt like I was about to pass out. My entire body started to shake. At that moment I was as scared of that bitch as little kids are of monsters in the closet. I didn't want to talk anymore, and I definitely didn't want her to touch me. But as a man, I didn't show it. I held that shit in, and she never knew what I was feeling. I'd never spoken to someone who I was interested in who told me she was HIV positive. It was always through a friend of a friend that you knew an HIV-positive person. We continued to talk for about another hour or so. I also learned that this chick was divorced from her husband who knew she had HIV before they got married. He didn't have it at the time and he still married her. Crazy, right? Toward the end of the conversation, she asked flat out if I could deal with someone like her, knowing her situation. I had to politely tell her, "No, I don't think I could." After that, she got up and we said our good-byes. After she left, my fear turned to relief because I thought in my younger days, I would have fucked her without a second thought. But being older and more experienced I was able to ask the right questions and potentially avoid a life-ending situation. I'm not saying that she wouldn't have told me about her status before we had sex, but what if she didn't? Back in the day I wouldn't have asked.

She happened to be one of the nice ones, but there are malicious people out there who are trying to spread this disease to anyone they can. Make sure you use protection at all times. Make sure you ask every potential partner what his HIV/STD status is. If he has a problem with answering questions about his HIV/STD status or getting tested or if he gives you a hard time about getting tested or retested, then dump his ass immediately and don't ever call again. Delete the phone number from your cell, delete the email address, and stop all contact. Forget that muthafucka ever existed because it's just not worth it. Even if he tells you his status is negative, get tested anyway. If it's negative, then he shouldn't have a problem getting tested again. Try to get paperwork if you can.

Make sure you and your partner get tested before you have sex. I don't care if you're both virgins, *get tested.* And get tested regularly, which is every three to six months. Even if you're not having sex, get tested. Since this Bill Clinton/Monica Lewinski incident, where in a court of law, Bill potentially redefined sex on the stand. Since then a lot of people want to try to reclassify what sex is. So like I said, even if you think you're not having sex, get tested. Once you get to an age where you can go to a clinic and get tested on your own, do it. There is no good reason not to get tested. The tests are free, and it only takes twenty minutes. If you don't abide by anything else in this book, at the bare minimum remember this: **GET TESTED!** Protect yourself, your family, and your future children because nobody is going to do it for you.

20

A CLOSING WORD

What! You made it to the end? I can't believe it. You must definitely be a woman who is eager to learn and is willing to change her way of thinking, because you know there's some harsh language and bone-chilling truth and criticisms in the previous pages. Did you laugh? Did you cry? Did you get upset? Did you feel like throwing up? Did you get that empty feeling in the pit of your stomach when something within the pages described you? It's okay. You're done now, and you can relax. I don't want you to leave with the attitude that I hate or dislike women because I don't. I love women. I was raised by women. I didn't write this book to degrade or disrespect women. I wrote the book to educate them. I wanted women to understand what the real deal is from a man's point of view—what men are thinking and how we feel.

From this point on, if you put down the book after you've read it and have the same attitude as before you picked it up or have a worse attitude because of it, then you haven't learned anything. When and if I ever have a daughter, I want her to be able to understand how men think so she won't get used. I want her to be able to understand men and how to get one when the time is right. I'm trying to do the same for the women who read this book. Be informed and know what's going on. Don't resort to blaming other people for your downfalls. A responsible person takes a hundred percent responsibility for his or her actions. If you view things this way, then you will take a look at yourself and your actions before you begin to blame others. You won't start to blame men because you can't get one. You'll ask yourself what is the cause of you not being able to get a man. By reading the information within this book, you can see it's not hard to get a man. The question is whether you really want to do what it takes to get one; whether you are listening to bad advice from your single, frustrated girlfriends who deep down inside really don't want you to have a man because they're afraid your friendship with them will change.

Regardless of what you may think of me or this book, I didn't write it to create further division between the African-American male and female. I wrote it, in part, to try to close the gap between the two and also to therapeutically vent my frustration with the way African-American males and females interact with one another. I also didn't want to turn this book into a history lesson, but I cannot effectively complete it without mentioning the profound effect that history and slavery have had on the way that African Americans deal with one another daily. A lot of the problems that affect the African-American community today are a direct result of the effects of mental and physical slavery. Even the problems that are causing us not to be able to come together and change the situation can be attributed to slavery.

African Americans have systematically been raped mentally, spiritually, and physically of their history, religion, and culture. Unless a dam is built to stop this behemoth Niagara Falls flow of misinformation, African Americans won't have to worry about the division between the sexes because we won't be here to see the end result. We will just become absorbed into society through miscegenation much like we were in South America. There are three very important things that African Americans need to understand before they can awake from their current vegetative state.

PLEADING FOR EQUALITY FROM THE RACE THAT OPPRESSED YOU IS AN EXERCISE IN FUTILITY. It's like giving an insect, a dog, or piece of garbage constitutional rights. For you to be equal to them in their minds is an impossibility. This is because racism goes far beyond skin color. Let me explain. Back when Europeans were raping our female ancestors, sometimes an offspring was born from this sexual assault. Often these offspring had more European features than African, so much so that they could "pass"—what they called it back then which means pass for White. While these Africans were passing for White they would be treated as any other European during that time. However if it ever became known that one of their parents was Black, they would be treated just as any African was treated, even if they had more pale skin, blond, blue-eyed features than their oppressor.

NO DEITY OR HEAVENLY BEING IS COMING TO SAVE YOU. Stop waiting for the sky to open up and for some extinction-level event to occur because it's not going to happen. You must take it upon yourself to do something about your own situation. No God in any religious text will ever intervene in your life no matter how pathetic your situation. Whatever you want to happen in life, you must make happen. Get off your ass and do something! Stop being happy and complacent with the scraps that are thrown to you. If you're just sitting around and waiting for some heavenly gift to drop in your lap to miraculously fix your own situation and you aren't making efforts to contribute to the betterment of your community and your people, then you deserve to get fucked in the ass with no Vaseline because you obviously like it.

WE NEED TO RECLAIM WHAT HAS BEEN LOST—SANKOFA. We don't need to do this by waiting for an outside influence to do it for us. We need to do it ourselves. The following books should be required reading for all Africans and African Americans and all cultures of African descent: *The African Origin of Civilization* by Dr. Cheikh Anta Diop, *They Came Before Columbus* by Dr. Ivan Van Sertima, *The Destruction of Black Civilization* by Chancellor Williams, *What They Never Told You in History Class* by Indus Khamit-Kush, *The Black Holocaust for Beginners* by S.E. Anderson, and *Christopher Columbus and The Afrikan Holocaust: Slavery and the Rise of European Capitalism* by Dr. John Henrik Clarke.

These books will give you the basic foundation and the truth concerning African-American history and culture. Please don't stop there. Also research the teachings of Dr. Yosef Ben-Jochannan, Dr. Carter G. Woodson, and my spiritual Father, The Sword of Allah, Dr. Khallid Abdul Muhammad. After you've done that, then keep going. There is plenty more Black history and knowledge to be gained even beyond these great men, revolutionaries, scholars, and historians. Remember, no other culture will ever effectively teach you the real truth about your own history and culture. This is something you must do for yourself, your family, and your children.

GLOSSARY

The below definitions may have several different meanings, but for the purpose of brevity I've defined the terms only as they are used in this book.

ANGRY SISTA SYNDROME *(as described by Jamal Sharif)*—a Black woman who is angry at all men because of her failed relationships, improper advice from her single female friends, and mistakes she's made with men

BLANK—an incorrect phone number

BOOGERBEAR—a fat woman, an ugly woman, an undesirable woman; also known as Bigfoot, Busted, Monkey Mouth, Mudduck, Porker, Silverback Gorilla, Scallywag, Sasquatch, Sausage Eater, Sausage Queen, Skank, Trollope, Trout Mouth, Wookie, Yeti

BOTTOM BITCH—usually the prostitute that brings in the most money and the one the pimp trusts the most

BOUNCE—to leave, a quick exit

BUN UP—make a woman your girlfriend, a couple

COCK BLOCK—when a man or woman stops potential action from the opposite sex

CONSCIOUS—having knowledge of self, knowledge of one's own history, culture, customs, and religion

DYKE—a lesbian

FAGELA—Italian slang for faggot

HIT—to have sex, *(to hit it)*

HOLLA—to talk to

IN HER FEELINGS—upset, angry, or melancholy

JUMPSTREET—the very beginning

LIKE THAT—all that, something or someone who is considered quality, good, exciting

OKEY-DOKE—trick, ruse, con, scam, hoax, deception

PHAT—**P**retty **H**ot **A**nd **T**empting; sexy, nice figure; associated with the body of a female, not the face

PLAY—attention from someone, interest

SEXCAPADE—a no-holds-barred sexual extravaganza

THE GAME—interaction between males and females, mental intercourse

TWAKA—the butt or vagina of a female

UNCONSCIOUS—having no knowledge of self, no knowledge of one's own history, culture, customs, and religion; a modern-day slave or walking zombie

WACK—weak, dumb, good for nothing, no good

WIFE BEATER—a plain white tank top; named for the frequency with which it appears on an individual who has been involved in televised domestic violence

WIFEY—a man's wife or a female he's currently seeing who has the most potential to be his wife

YAM—a Black person who acts White; also known as an Uncle Tom, a coconut, an Oreo, a Clarence Thomas

YAP—mouth

ABOUT THE AUTHOR

Dante Moore is a single father, and a native of Washington D.C., who attended Morgan State University. His calm demeanor enabled him to gain a myriad of female friends. In dealing with these friends, and family members, he came to understand that what they were looking for in men was right in front of them but that they didn't possess the necessary skills to obtain it. Through countless conversations, debates, forums and real-life events he was able to put together his first set of thoughts and instructions to the opposite sex. In doing so Dante noticed a mass amount of interest from females outside of his immediate circle, so he consolidated his thoughts and views on relationships and other topics and put together what is now known as *The Re-Education of the Female*. You may email the author at TheReeducator@yahoo.com or visit his website at www.thereeducation.com

DISCUSSION GUIDE

1. What did you think about the title of the book?
2. How does the title of the book compare to the content?
3. Did you feel that the book fulfilled your expectations? Were you disappointed?
4. Did you enjoy the book? Why? Why not?
5. How did the book compare to other books in the same genre?
6. How realistic was the book?
7. What are the things the author says females need to be re-educated about?
8. What does the author see as traits of a good man?
9. Do you agree with the author's assessment of first date expenses? Why? Why not?
10. Do you believe the author's viewpoint is affected by his experiences alone? Or could there be some general truths to what the author has written?
11. How do the topics discussed throughout the book pertain to your relationships and/or dating experiences?
12. What myths and/or misconceptions about men, if any, did this book dispel for you?
13. Do you think any of your past relationships have failed as a result of the issues the author reveals in the book?
14. How can you apply the concepts in the book to your current or future relationships?
15. Did the book end the way you expected?
16. Did you learn anything? Why? Why not?
17. Would you recommend this book to other readers? To your close friends?
18. Would you recommend this book to a friend who is having relationship problems? Why? Why not?